THE YELLOWSTONE
FLY-FISHING GUIDE

THE YELLOWSTONE FLY-FISHING GUIDE

CRAIG MATHEWS AND CLAYTON MOLINERO

THE LYONS PRESS

Printed in the United States of America

10 9 8 7 6 5 4 3 2

Maps and illustrations by Rod Walinchus, copyright © 1997
Design by Barry T. Kerrigan, Desktop Miracles Inc., Addison, Texas

Library of Congress Cataloging-in-Publication Data

Matthews, Craig
    The Yellowstone fly-fishing guide / Craig Matthews and Clayton Molinero.
        p. cm.
    Includes index.
    ISBN 1-55821-545-X
    1. Fly fishing—Yellowstone National Park—Guidebooks.   2. Yellowstone National Park—Guidebooks.   I. Molinero, Clayton.   II. Title.
SH464.Y45M38   1997
799.1'24'0978752—dc21   97-6966
                                                                                            CIP

CONTENTS

ACKNOWLEDGMENTS

We'd like to thank our many friends who have shared their knowledge of Yellowstone Park waters. We'd also like to thank those who contributed photographs: Linda and Andre Altans, Dan Daufel, Doug Daufel, Larry Dech, John Juracek, Harry Mayo, Rowan Nyman, and Phil Takatsuno. A special thanks to Howard Back, Ray Bergman, Charlie Brooks, and Nick Lyons, whose narratives inspired us to make Yellowstone waters our home waters.

PREFACE

A fly-fishing guide to Yellowstone Park has long been needed. Yellowstone has more than a hundred lakes and a thousand miles of streams, and the majority of this water is overlooked in favor of a few popular and easily accessible places. We want to make anglers aware of all of Yellowstone's fishing opportunities.

Accurate and reliable information about Park waters has been hard to come by in the past. The information in this book comes through personal experience; we've worn out our share of boots on wild goose chases. Together, we've spent more than 30 years exploring and fishing these waters. We hope you'll find this guide useful for planning and for fishing Yellowstone.

Yellowstone Lake

INTRODUCTION

It's a clear, chilly September night in the little meadow. A bull elk bugles his harem of cows together from across the river. A group of men huddled around a campfire are warming their hands and discussing how they can own and profit from the lands their expedition has discovered. As the argument cools, one man quietly stands, clears his throat, and says, "I don't approve of any of these plans. There should be no private ownership of any portion of this region; rather, the whole of it should be set aside as a national park, and each of us ought to make an effort to get this accomplished."

This was Judge Cornelius Hedges of Montana, a member of the 1870 Washburn Expedition sent to investigate rumors of a place called "Yellowstone." With rare foresight, the other expedition members agreed with Judge Hedges and saw Yellowstone's potential to yield more than self-serving economic gain. And thus was born the idea for a national park. In 1872, President Ulysses S. Grant formally proclaimed Yellowstone our first such park. Everyone who enjoys Yellowstone, Yosemite, Acadia, the Great Smoky Mountains, or any of the other jewels in our national park system today owes a deep debt of gratitude to the Washburn Expedition of 1870.

Yellowstone Park comprises approximately 2,221,000 acres spread across the spine of the Rocky Mountains, where the states of Wyoming, Montana, and Idaho come together. The mountains are split by the Continental Divide, which sends Yellowstone Park water to both the East and West Coasts. The Madison, Gallatin, and Yellowstone Rivers flow into the Atlantic through the Gulf of Mexico, while the Snake, Lewis, and Bechler Rivers drain into the Pacific. There are over a hundred lakes and a thousand miles of streams here; nowhere in the world are so many public rivers and streams found in such a small area.

1

FISHING YELLOWSTONE

Seven varieties of gamefish live in Yellowstone: cutthroat, rainbow, brown, brook, and lake trout, along with grayling and mountain whitefish. Only cutthroats, grayling, and mountain whitefish are native to the Park.

In the 1890s, any lake, stream, pond, river, or slough that held water was stocked with fish. Little was known then about fisheries management; many of these places could not support self-sustaining populations and returned to their former barren state. Those that could support fish retain wild populations to this day. The last fish were stocked in Yellowstone in the mid-1950s.

REGULATIONS

The Park's general fishing season begins in May, on the Saturday of the Memorial Day weekend, and it ends on the first Sunday in November, inclusive. There are some exceptions: Yellowstone Lake opens June 15. The Yellowstone River and its tributaries, from the Chittenden Bridge upstream (south) to the lake, open July 15. Other lakes and streams have special opening dates that may vary from the general season. Some waters are permanently closed to fishing to protect wildlife and geothermal features. Before fishing, always check the park service's booklet, *Fishing Regulations for Yellowstone National Park.*

Anyone 16 years and older must have a valid Yellowstone National Park permit to fish in the Park. Those 13 to 15 years old must obtain a special, free permit. Children 12 years and younger may fish without a permit but must comply with all Yellowstone Park regulations. Fishing permits are available at the main entrance gates, ranger stations, and stores within the Park as well as fly-fishing shops in the surrounding communities. All fees collected stay within the fisheries program in the Park.

If you plan to use a boat or float tube in the Park you'll need a boating permit. These can be purchased at many ranger stations, backcountry offices, or Park entrances. Check the "Boats–Float Tubes" section within the Park's fishing regulations booklet for specific locations where boating permits can be purchased.

WHEN TO COME

It's a typical spring in Yellowstone National Park. Although the Memorial Day weekend and the season opener are in sight, ice still covers Yellowstone Lake, and snow is still up to the eaves of the outhouses at the

Buffalo Ford picnic area on the Yellowstone River. With the average elevation at nearly 7,000 feet, summer comes late and winter arrives early.

The first river to clear from snowmelt is the Firehole; it's often the only game in the Park on the opener, and each May a group of Firehole River regulars eagerly awaits the Memorial Day weekend. The Firehole usually offers great dry-fly fishing during afternoon mayfly hatches and continues to do so until the end of June. By the second week of June, the Gibbon and Madison Rivers drop and clear, the ice comes off Yellowstone Lake, and the fishing season is under way for other waters. One by one the Park's rivers run clear of snowmelt, and most become fishable by July 4. Usually, the last rivers to clear are the Yellowstone and Lamar in early July.

There is no "best" time to fish Yellowstone Park. Each month of the short season offers its own style of best fishing. From the season opener in late May through the end of June, the best places to fish are the Firehole, Gibbon, Madison, and Lewis Rivers, and both Yellowstone and Trout Lakes, when they open on June 15.

In July, all waters become fishable in the Park, including the small streams. Insect hatches are at their peak in July, and this is a favorite time for dry-fly fishers. The Firehole and Madison Rivers are two exceptions, however, because a combination of thermal water and summer heat raises their water temperatures into the 80s. Fishing is slow on these two rivers until water temperatures drop in early September. July and August are our fair-weather months, with the most consistent hatches and favorable stream conditions.

August is the best time for lake fishing in the Park. This is a great time to fish the backcountry lakes in Yellowstone, as the mosquitoes and biting flies thin. All rivers except the Firehole and Madison continue to fish well through the month. As the aquatic insect emergences wane, terrestrials play an increasingly important role in the trout diet. Imitations of grasshoppers, ants, crickets, and beetles are a mainstay in the angler's arsenal until the end of the season.

During the late season, September and October, only a few hatches remain. The big Green Drakes appear on the Lamar River and Slough Creek, along with tiny Blue-Winged Olives and midges. The Firehole and Madison Rivers become fishable again and produce excellent hatches of BWOs and midges. October is the best month to come if you want to catch the large migrating fish in the Madison and Lewis Rivers. As spawning time approaches and the weather becomes more winterlike, these big trout become aggressive and territorial, attacking baitfish imitations and other large streamer flies.

WHERE TO STAY

There are camping and lodging facilities both inside the Park and at the gate communities of Cooke City, Gardiner, and West Yellowstone, Montana, as well as at Cody and Jackson, Wyoming, which are all about an hour away. Reservations for lodging should be made well in advance of your trip, particularly for the peak months of July, August, and September. For instance, the Park's Old Faithful Inn is often booked a full six months in advance. Call (307) 344-7311 for lodging reservations within the Park.

If you're planning an overnight stay in the backcountry, you'll need a permit. Campsites are designated through a backcountry reservation system. Policies and conditions change yearly, so contact the Park for current information: Backcountry Office, P.O. Box 168, Yellowstone National Park, WY 82190; or call (307) 344-2160.

WHAT TO BRING

Each gate community offers a selection of fly shops and guide services. Make it a point to check with these local experts regarding current stream conditions and hatches. First-time visitors should spend a day or two with a knowledgeable guide; this can save you a lot of gas and boot leather.

We recommend an 8½- or 9-foot rod balanced for a 4- to 6-weight line. A floating weight-forward or double-taper line will handle most situations. Full-sinking lines are helpful on lakes, and sink-tip lines are often used when fishing streamers or big nymphs in the fall.

Bears, Backcountry, and Anglers

Yellowstone is bear country, and there is no guarantee of your safety. Bears often utilize trails, streams, and lakeshores. Entry into some areas may be restricted; check with a ranger for specific bear management information. Traveling alone in bear country is not recommended. Make enough noise to make your presence known to bears. If you should encounter a bear, give it plenty of room, detour if possible, or wait for the bear to move on. If a bear should charge or attack and the situation allows, climb a tree. If you are caught by a bear, try playing dead. Do not run; this may excite the bear. Carefully read all bear country guidelines and regulations and be prepared for any situation.

From *Fishing Regulations for Yellowstone National Park*

Felt-soled, chest-high waders are the choice of most Yellowstone anglers. Lightweight waders made of Gore-Tex or microfibers are convenient for packing along on backcountry trips. Neoprene waders are required in colder weather, especially when tubing lakes or fishing in the fall.

Never go fishing in Yellowstone without rain gear, sunscreen, sunglasses, bug dope, and a hat. Backcountry users may want to have a can of bear repellent (pepper spray) handy and hang bells on their packs. Although we single out bears, *all* animals in the Park are wild and should be given a wide berth and proper respect. We have seen more visitors put up trees by elk, bison, and moose than by all the bears combined.

HATCHES

Whenever possible we refer to insects by their common names. When no common name is available, we use an insect's scientific name.

In the accompanying sidebar you'll find an overall emergence table that will give you an idea when to expect various insects throughout the Park. In the chapters to come, major lakes and rivers where hatches are important are also accompanied by specific emergence tables. Below is some broadly useful information about insect activity in the park.

Mayflies are most vulnerable and available to trout while hatching and during egg laying and subsequent spinner falls.

Baetis (Blue-Winged Olives, or BWOs) emerge best from 11 A.M. to 4 P.M. on overcast, rainy, or snowy days. The cooler the day, the later the hatch.

Rhithrogena spinners are sometimes important on calm, warm evenings during July and August.

Pale Morning Duns (PMDs) generally emerge at the most comfortable time of day: noon to 1 P.M. on snowy days; 9 to 11 A.M. on sunny, warm days. Spinner falls are best on calm, warm mornings, 9 to 11 A.M., and again during the evening, 7 to 10 P.M.

Green Drakes emerge from 10 A.M. to 1 P.M. Fall Green Drakes come off from 1 to 4 P.M. Spinner falls (seldom encountered) occur from 7 to 9 A.M.

Brown Drakes hatch from 7 to 10 P.M.; spinner falls coincide with emergences.

Flavs emerge on clear days from 8 to 9 P.M. In cloudy, rainy conditions look for them from 1 P.M. on. Spinner falls occur from 7 to 9 P.M.

Gray Drakes on Slough Creek emerge sporadically all day long, beginning as early as 8 A.M. Spinner activity is better coordinated and goes from 9 A.M. until noon. On the Yellowstone River, spinner falls occur twice each day, 8 to 10 A.M. and 7 to 9 P.M.

Callibaetis duns emerge on lakes from 10 A.M. to 2 P.M.; spinner falls occur from 11 A.M. to 3 P.M.

Tricorythodes show on the Madison River between 10 A.M. and noon; spinners are more important than duns.

Pink Ladies hatch from 4 to 7 P.M.

Attenella margarita duns and spinners can appear together from 9 to 11 A.M. Spinners may fall on warm, calm evenings as well.

Serratella tibialis duns come off between 11 A.M. and 3 P.M., with spinner falls from 7 to 9 P.M.

Heptagenia duns, when found, emerge between 1 and 5 P.M. Spinners fall best on warm, calm evenings.

Caddis emerge best on warm, calm evenings. Egg-laying activity usually occurs at the same time. However, in their peak periods caddis may also be found laying eggs in the morning. Trout recognize both emerging and egg-laying periods and feed best during these two events.

There are two important exceptions to this:

Lepidostoma on the Gibbon River often emerge during the early afternoon on cloudy days.

Hesperophylax caddis on the Yellowstone River usually emerge from 8 to 9 A.M.

Stoneflies, such as the **Salmonfly** and **Golden Stonefly,** have their strongest egg-laying periods on warm, windy, sunny days from 10 A.M. to 6 P.M. These clumsy fliers are most available to trout when they bounce on the water while depositing their eggs.

Little Yellow Stones lay eggs in the late afternoon and early evening, 3 to 8 P.M.

Damselflies prefer warm, sunny mornings and afternoons, 10 A.M. to 3 P.M. Look for migrating nymphs and newly hatched adults along the shoreline.

Midges are important throughout the Park. Be prepared to fish midges at any time of day, on any water.

Midge

INSECT EMERGENCES

MAYFLIES

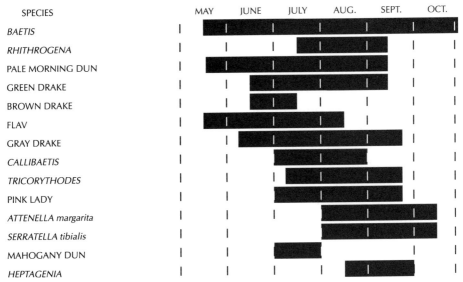

SPECIES	MAY	JUNE	JULY	AUG.	SEPT.	OCT.
BAETIS						
RHITHROGENA						
PALE MORNING DUN						
GREEN DRAKE						
BROWN DRAKE						
FLAV						
GRAY DRAKE						
CALLIBAETIS						
TRICORYTHODES						
PINK LADY						
ATTENELLA margarita						
SERRATELLA tibialis						
MAHOGANY DUN						
HEPTAGENIA						

CADDIS

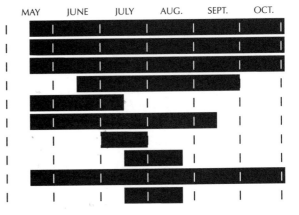

SPECIES	MAY	JUNE	JULY	AUG.	SEPT.	OCT.
BRACHYCENTRUS						
HYDROPSYCHE						
HELICOPSYCHE						
GLOSSOSOMA						
OECETIS						
LEPIDOSTOMA						
ARCTOPSYCHE						
HESPEROPHYLAX						
RHYACOPHILA						
MICRASEMA						

OTHER INSECTS

SPECIES	MAY	JUNE	JULY	AUG.	SEPT.	OCT.
SALMONFLY						
GOLDEN STONEFLY						
LITTLE YELLOW STONE						
DAMSELFLIES						
MIDGES						
TERRESTRIALS						

THE LAKES AND PONDS OF YELLOWSTONE

At this writing, Yellowstone's lakes and ponds remain an untapped resource and largely unexplored, visited by only a handful of Yellowstone regulars. It's a mystery why so many anglers are reluctant to give lake fishing a try.

Yellowstone's stillwaters offer solitude, a pleasant change of pace from the sometimes crowded rivers, and a chance to see the Park as few others do. The lakes feature fishing for all trout species, and they provide your best opportunity to land a trophy trout or one of the seldom-seen grayling. The lakes have periods of fine dry-fly fishing to emerging insects. When insects aren't hatching, there's great fishing with subsurface flies. Each season we seem to spend more and more time exploring the lakes of Yellowstone. Remember that if you're bringing in a boat or float tube, you'll need a permit for your watercraft as well as a fishing permit.

HOW TO USE THIS BOOK

The Park is divided into four sections by a network of roads called the Loop Roads.

1. **Northwest:** *West Entrance* (West Yellowstone, Montana)—Madison Junction—Norris Junction—Canyon Junction—Tower Junction—Mammoth—*North Entrance* (Gardiner, Montana).
2. **Northeast:** *East Entrance*—Fishing Bridge—Canyon Junction—Tower Junction—Mammoth—*North Entrance* (Gardiner, Montana). Cody, Wyoming, is one hour east of YNP's East Entrance.
3. **Southeast:** *South Entrance*—West Thumb—Fishing Bridge—*East Entrance*. Jackson, Wyoming, is one hour south of YNP's South Entrance.
4. **Southwest:** *South Entrance*—West Thumb—Canyon Junction—Norris Junction—Madison Junction—*West Entrance* (West Yellowstone, Montana).

This book is divided into the same four sections. Each begins with an overview of the area. Waters are listed alphabetically under two headings: *Rivers and Streams* and *Lakes and Ponds*. The major rivers and lakes are discussed in detail and are followed by an emergence chart and a list of fly patterns. With each listing is a reference to the appropriate map and brief instructions for road/trail access. Fishless waters are not always on the maps.

THE MAPS

Our maps are intended as a guide to locate trout waters within the Park. *They are not substitutes for topographical maps.* When you're hiking the backcountry, we feel a topo map and compass are mandatory to ensure your safety.

The maps for each of this book's four sections are divided by major watersheds, which allows them to be as complete as possible. Section 1, *Northwest,* contains four maps covering the four major watersheds within this section: the Madison, Gallatin, Gardner, and Gibbon Rivers. Section 2, *Northeast,* contains three maps covering the Yellowstone River, the Canyon, and the Lamar River. Section 3, *Southeast,* contains two maps covering Yellowstone Lake and the Thorofare region. Section 4, *Southwest,* contains four maps covering the Firehole River, Nez Perce Creek, Lewis Lake, and the Bechler River.

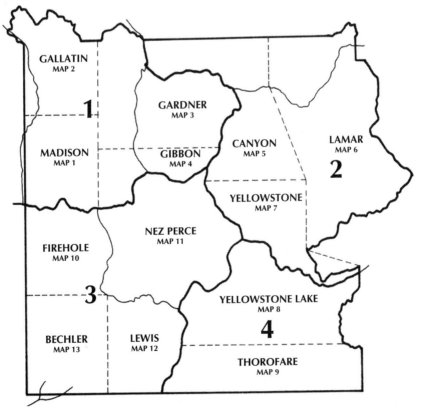

ICONS

With each listed water we've included symbols to help you choose where to go. These quickly indicate what species of fish you'll find, whether you can drive to the water or must hike, and whether the area has a lot of bear or moose activity.

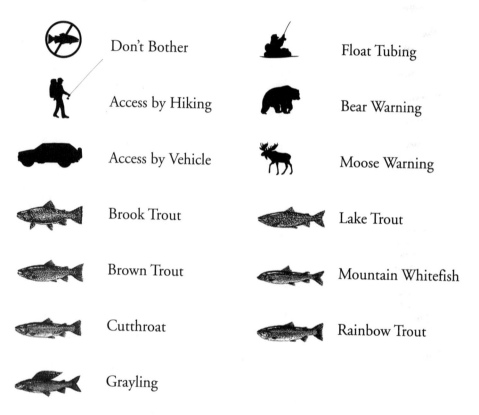

	Don't Bother		Float Tubing
	Access by Hiking		Bear Warning
	Access by Vehicle		Moose Warning
	Brook Trout		Lake Trout
	Brown Trout		Mountain Whitefish
	Cutthroat		Rainbow Trout
	Grayling		

THE FUTURE

Fishing in Yellowstone Park is better than it has ever been. Over the past 40 years the gutsy management of the Park's fisheries has been an unqualified success story. Ineffective and costly hatchery programs were eliminated in the 1950s. Restrictive limits and catch-and-release were introduced in the 1970s. These policies have produced the best wild trout fishery in the world. Simply put, Yellowstone's rivers and lakes are better managed than any others in the world.

In 1994 Yellowstone Park officials introduced a fee permit policy to help pay the increased costs of protecting and enhancing this world-class fishery. Moneys from these fishing permits stay in Yellowstone and go directly to work for the Park's fisheries program.

At this writing, native populations of Yellowstone cutthroats may be threatened by the presence of predatory lake trout in both the Yellowstone River and Yellowstone Lake. With public support and an innovative lake-trout control program, fisheries officials are optimistic about the future of Yellowstone cutthroats.

Yellowstone Park and its fishery are a national treasure. As we use this renewable resource, we should apply the same foresight as did the Park founders over a century ago. Yellowstone is one of the few places left in the world that is wild and free. We must all do our part to maintain this last best place for future generations.

The Fires of 1988

At the time, the fires of 1988 seemed a devastating blow to the Yellowstone Park we were used to fishing. Like most people, we were uncomfortable with change, and these fires were beyond change! But nearly a decade later we can see the positive effect the fires have had on the ecosystem.

There has been an increase in life in the Park. There are new trees, more wildflowers, and increased populations of birds, bison, bears, and elk—all due to the new growth and habitat provided by the fires. The Park's waters have been enriched by nutrients from the fires. Insect numbers and fish sizes seem better than ever. The panic of 1988 proved unwarranted. Once again, nature has taken care of itself.

1
NORTHWEST

MADISON, GALLATIN, GARDNER, AND GIBBON RIVERS

This section contains four of the Park's most popular rivers: the Madison, Gallatin, Gardner, and Gibbon. All are easily accessible by car and rated blue-ribbon trout streams. The U.S. Fish and Wildlife Service rates the Madison the world's second best trout stream; the Yellowstone River is first.

In *The Living River* (Nick Lyons Books, New York, 1979), Charles Brooks described the Madison River as the world's largest chalkstream. He wrote that its waters are rich in calcium bicarbonate—the mineral most crucial to aquatic life and the base of the food chain that nourishes the wild trout for which this river is world famous.

The Shoshone called the Gallatin River *Cut-tuh-o'-gwa*, or "swift river." The Gallatin is this and much more. Its icy waters hold a diverse and abundant insect population, providing plenty of food for three species of trout, mountain whitefish, and the rare Montana grayling.

The Gardner River is often overlooked in favor of more publicized waters, and local anglers like to keep it under their hats. The river offers something for everyone—meadow water for the dry-fly angler, and rough-and-tumble stretches for the nymph fisher. Attractor flies and terrestrials provide fun fishing all summer long.

The secrets to the Gibbon River are under lock, and only the patient and observant angler will learn the combination. Deep pools and undercuts harbor large brown trout and the elusive grayling. Riffles and pockets hide rainbows and brook trout. This stream gives the fly fisher the choice of an easy or a very challenging day.

Good fishing is where you find it, and numerous small streams and lakes in the northwestern quadrant of the Park are available to those willing to explore the backcountry.

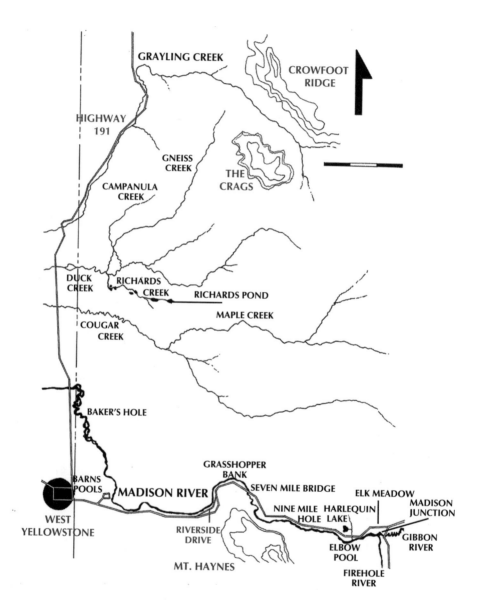

Map 1 — Madison River

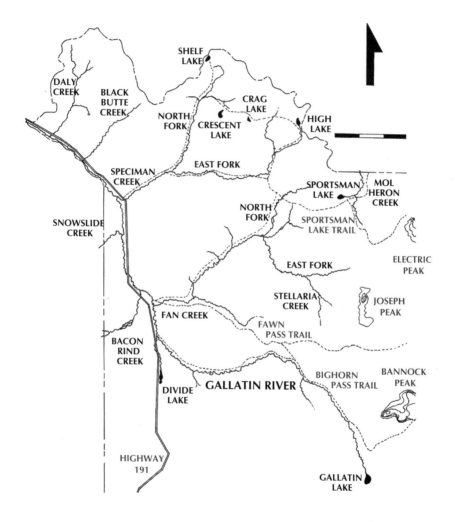

Map 2 — Gallatin River

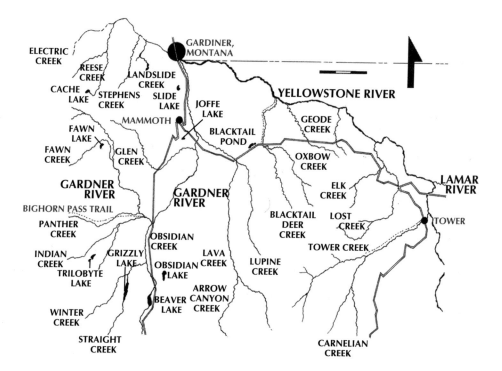

ELECTRIC
CREEK

GARDINER,
MONTANA

REESE
CREEK

LANDSLIDE
CREEK

CACHE
LAKE

STEPHENS
CREEK

SLIDE
LAKE

JOFFE
LAKE

YELLOWSTONE RIVER

MAMMOTH

BLACKTAIL
POND

GEODE
CREEK

FAWN
LAKE

GLEN
CREEK

OXBOW
CREEK

FAWN
CREEK

GARDNER
RIVER

GARDNER
RIVER

LAMAR
RIVER

BIGHORN PASS TRAIL

ELK
CREEK

PANTHER
CREEK

OBSIDIAN
CREEK

BLACKTAIL
DEER
CREEK

LOST
CREEK

TOWER

INDIAN
CREEK

GRIZZLY
LAKE

LAVA
CREEK

LUPINE
CREEK

TOWER CREEK

TRILOBYTE
LAKE

OBSIDIAN
LAKE

ARROW
CANYON
CREEK

WINTER
CREEK

BEAVER
LAKE

STRAIGHT
CREEK

CARNELIAN
CREEK

Map 3 — Gardner River

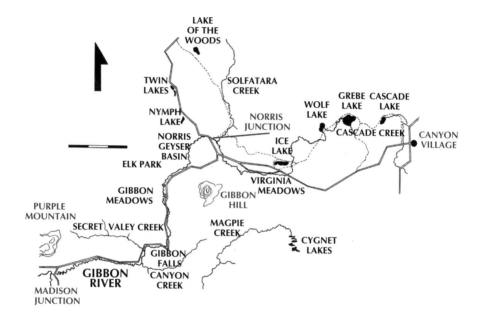

LAKE
OF THE
WOODS

TWIN
LAKES

SOLFATARA
CREEK

GREBE CASCADE
LAKE   LAKE

WOLF
LAKE

NYMPH
LAKE

NORRIS
JUNCTION

CASCADE CREEK

CANYON
VILLAGE

NORRIS
GEYSER
BASIN

ICE
LAKE

ELK PARK

VIRGINIA
MEADOWS

GIBBON
MEADOWS

GIBBON
HILL

GIBBON
MEADOWS

PURPLE
MOUNTAIN

SECRET VALEY CREEK

MAGPIE
CREEK

CYGNET
LAKES

GIBBON
FALLS

**GIBBON
RIVER**

CANYON
CREEK

MADISON
JUNCTION

Map 4 — Gibbon River

RIVERS AND STREAMS

Arrow Canyon Creek (Map 3)

BROOK TROUT

This small tributary to the headwaters of Lava Creek can be reached by following Lava Creek upstream for 8 miles from the Lava Creek picnic area via the Mammoth-Tower Highway. There is no trail, and the fishing is only fair for small brook trout averaging 6 inches.

Bacon Rind Creek (Map 2)

CUTTHROAT • RAINBOW TROUT

This small, icy tributary to the Gallatin River is between Mile Markers 22 and 23 on Highway 191 north of West Yellowstone. A trail along the hillside follows the stream up the valley, avoiding downfalls and brushy areas. Cutthroat and rainbow trout attack attractor dry flies and terrestrial patterns during the late summer. The best fishing is in the pockets and pools between the riffles, with the trout averaging 9 inches. This stream receives heavy fishing pressure when it clears of snowmelt in July.

Black Butte Creek (Map 2)

This tiny tributary to the Gallatin River appears incapable of supporting a fishable population of trout.

Blacktail Deer Creek (Map 3)

BROOK TROUT

This lovely tributary to the Yellowstone River is 7 miles east of Mammoth on the Mammoth-Tower Highway. Blacktail Deer Trail follows the creek along the 4-mile stretch downstream to the Yellowstone. The fishing is excellent for richly colored brook trout in the 9- to 10-inch range. During terrestrial time, July through September, the trout ravenously attack grasshopper, beetle, and cricket patterns. Easy access and good fishing make this one of our most popular small streams. The fishing on the upstream side of the highway is also good and receives a lot less pressure.

Campanula Creek (Map 1)

BROOK TROUT

This small tributary enters Duck Creek from the north, a mile east of the Gneiss Creek Trailhead. It contains brook trout averaging 6 inches, but if beavers have been active building dams and ponds, it can hold larger fish.

Canyon Creek (Map 4)

BROOK TROUT • RAINBOW TROUT • GRAYLING

Canyon Creek is a small tributary to the Gibbon River located below Gibbon Falls, across the river from the Gibbon River picnic area. Seven-inch brook and rainbow trout, along with a small population of Montana grayling, inhabit its undercuts. The fires of 1988 resulted in a lot of downed timber in the area, making both travel and fishing difficult.

Carnelian Creek (Map 3)

BROOK TROUT • RAINBOW TROUT

This small tributary to Tower Creek, located about 4 miles upstream of the campground at Tower Falls, offers good fishing for brook and rainbow trout of around 8 inches, but it runs through country heavily used by grizzly bears.

Cascade Creek (Map 4)

CUTTHROAT • H M B

Cutthroat trout that average 9 inches are plentiful in this small creek, which parallels most of the Howard Eaton Trail, from the trailhead to the creek's origins in Cascade

Lake, about 2½ miles. The trail to Cascade Lake begins ½ mile west of Canyon Junction on the north side of the road. Many anglers taking the trail up to the lake end up spending the day sidetracked by the creek.

Cougar Creek (Map 1)

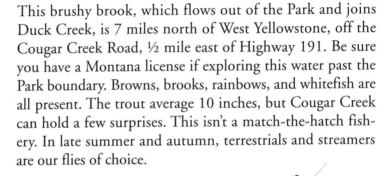

BROOK TROUT • BROWN TROUT • RAINBOW TROUT • MOUNTAIN WHITEFISH

This brushy brook, which flows out of the Park and joins Duck Creek, is 7 miles north of West Yellowstone, off the Cougar Creek Road, ½ mile east of Highway 191. Be sure you have a Montana license if exploring this water past the Park boundary. Browns, brooks, rainbows, and whitefish are all present. The trout average 10 inches, but Cougar Creek can hold a few surprises. This isn't a match-the-hatch fishery. In late summer and autumn, terrestrials and streamers are our flies of choice.

Daly Creek (Map 2)

CUTTHROAT • RAINBOW TROUT

This small, cold tributary to the Gallatin River parallels the popular Daly Creek Trail and is located just south of Mile Marker 30, 30 miles north of West Yellowstone on Highway 191. Cutthroat and rainbow trout averaging 8 inches are plentiful at times; they can be taken on attractor dry flies and terrestrials during the dog days of summer.

Duck Creek (Map 1)

BROOK TROUT • BROWN TROUT • RAINBOW TROUT

Duck Creek is good-sized meadow stream located 8 miles north of West Yellowstone, then east off Highway 191 on the Duck Creek Road. Formed by the waters of Campanula, Gneiss, and Richards Creeks, this fine stream meanders its way through country heavily populated by bear and moose. In spawning season, Duck Creek's small population of resident fish is bolstered by brown, brook, and rainbow trout averaging 16 inches that migrate from Montana's Hebgen Lake.

Pale Morning Duns and Gray and Green Drakes can bring the fish to the surface during June and early July. Terrestrials such as ants, beetles, and grasshoppers are a must in late summer. Look for mayfly activity on overcast days and terrestrial action on bright, sunny, and windy days.

Duck Creek is one of the few waters in Yellowstone Park that suffered as a result of the fires of 1988. However, the good water years of 1993, 1995, and 1996 are gradually reducing the heavy siltation caused by the fires, and necessary habitat for both resident and spawning trout is now available.

Fan Creek (Map 2)

BROWN TROUT • CUTTHROAT • RAINBOW TROUT

This tributary to the Gallatin River, located at Mile Marker 22, 22 miles north of West Yellowstone on Highway 191, is reached by taking the Fawn Pass Trail, then taking a left onto the Sportsman Lake Trail. A small meadow stream, Fan Creek holds healthy populations of cutthroat and rainbow trout, along with the occasional large brown. *Baetis,* Flavs, Green Drakes, and Pale Morning Duns are plentiful, and there are some caddis hatches. In late summer, terrestrials are good producers here.

Fan Creek

For such a small stream, Fan Creek holds trout that can be exceedingly selective and difficult to catch. Attractor flies work fine on most small streams, but here we recommend matching the hatch.

Gallatin River (Map 2)

BROOK TROUT • BROWN TROUT • CUTTHROAT • RAINBOW TROUT • GRAYLING • MOUNTAIN WHITEFISH

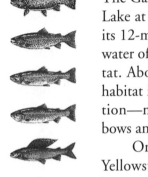

The Gallatin begins as an icy trickle leaving remote Gallatin Lake at nearly 10,000 feet in elevation. On the first half of its 12-mile journey downstream to Highway 191, the frigid water of the Gallatin provides little in the way of trout habitat. About halfway between the lake and the highway the habitat improves, but the river remains a small-fish proposition—mostly cutthroat and brook trout, with a few rainbows and browns.

Once in view of the highway, 20 miles north of West Yellowstone, the river develops more character. Willows begin to line the riverbank, and as the water meanders through them, undercut banks and weed beds begin to appear. Fish numbers and sizes increase proportionally with the improvement of the holding water and increase in insect life. The river is still ice cold here and is usually discolored by snowmelt until July 4. Immediately after clearing, both aquatic and terrestrial insect activity increase.

River access is easy all the way to the Park's north boundary, as the river flows parallel to the road. Numbered roadside mile markers are a quick way to identify your location. The river comes into view on the east side of the road at Mile Marker 20 and for the next 11 miles remains in the Park. (Keep in mind that the mile-marker number is the same regardless of your direction of travel.) Once you leave the Park near Mile Marker 31, your Yellowstone Park fishing permit is no longer valid; you'll need a Montana fishing license from here downstream.

This stretch of water is a pleasant mix of mountain freestone and meadow water, with enough undercut banks to house larger fish. Boulders, pockets, pools, and eddies

Gallatin River

combine to present a challenge to any angler, with enough variety to suit any mood or technique.

The Gallatin has a good population of rainbows, along with browns, cutthroats, grayling, and whitefish. This looks like classic rainbow water, and the average trout runs 11 to 12 inches. First-timers on the Gallatin are often surprised by browns twice that size, however. They're also surprised by where they hold. The browns are in the obvious deep runs, pockets, and undercuts, but they also turn up in water so shallow that their backs are out of the water. We relearn this lesson every year: Keep your eyes open for every inch of water. In the Gallatin, the big fish are often in small-fish water, and the small fish are where we think the big fish should be.

Because the Gallatin hosts an incredibly diverse insect population—more than 200 species of mayflies, caddis, and stoneflies—attractor flies are often more successful than match-the-hatch patterns. The notable exceptions are hatches of Pale Morning Duns, Flavs, and Green Drakes.

Rhyacophila

Last July at Moose Crossing, for example, the trout began refusing our blind-fished attractor dries in favor of Pale Morning Duns hatching against the far bank. When we switched to matching patterns, we were back in business.

The Gallatin is one of the premier terrestrial streams in Yellowstone. Overhanging grassy banks provide plenty of land-borne insects that drop or are blown into the water, and trout can't resist them. A 92-year-old local gal says, "Hoppers catch 'bows and beetles catch browns." She advises employing a tandem rig to cover both, and we enthusiastically agree.

SELECTED EMERGENCES

MAYFLIES

SPECIES	MAY	JUNE	JULY	AUG.	SEPT.	OCT.
BAETIS	██████████████████████████████████████					
PALE MORNING DUN			████████			
FLAV			████████			
GREEN DRAKE			██████			
PINK LADY			████████████			

CADDIS

SPECIES	MAY	JUNE	JULY	AUG.	SEPT.	OCT.
HYDROPSYCHE			████████████			
ARCTOPSYCHE			██████████			
RHYACOPHILA			██████████			

Many other caddis species are present, but these three predominate.

STONEFLIES

SPECIES	MAY	JUNE	JULY	AUG.	SEPT.	OCT.
SALMONFLY			█████			
GOLDEN STONEFLY		████████████				
LITTLE YELLOW STONE			████████████			

Salmonflies hatch sporadically in the Park.

TERRESTRIALS

SPECIES		MAY	JUNE	JULY	AUG.	SEPT.	OCT.
ANTS, BEETLES, CRICKETS, AND GRASSHOPPERS							

SELECTED FLY PATTERNS

MAYFLIES

BAETIS

    BAETIS NYMPH, #20

    BAETIS SPARKLE DUN, #20

PALE MORNING DUN (PMD)

    PHEASANT TAIL NYMPH, #16

    PMD SPARKLE DUN, #16

FLAV

    PHEASANT TAIL NYMPH, #14

    FLAV SPARKLE DUN, #14–#16

    ADAMS, #14–#16

GREEN DRAKE

    GREEN DRAKE EMERGER, #10–#12

    PARADRAKE, #10–#12

PINK LADY

    PINK LADY SOFT HACKLE, #16

    PINK LADY SPARKLE DUN, #16

CADDIS

    PEEKING CADDIS LARVA, #10–#14

    NICK'S SOFT HACKLE, #16

    X-CADDIS, OLIVE AND TAN, #14–#18

    ELK HAIR CADDIS AND KAUFMANN'S STIMULATOR, #12–#16

STONEFLIES

    KAUFMANN'S AMBER SEAL STONE NYMPH, #6–#10

    GEORGE'S BROWN STONE, #6–#10

    KAUFMANN'S YELLOW STIMULATOR, #6–#16

    LITTLE YELLOW STONEFLY, #14–#18

ATTRACTORS

    PRINCE NYMPH, #8–#16

    SERENDIPITY, BROWN, LIME, OLIVE, RED, CRYSTAL, #14–#18

    ROYAL TRUDE, H&L VARIANT, GOOFUS BUG, AND ROYAL WULFF, #12–#18

TERRESTRIALS

PARACHUTE ANT, #14–#18

FOAM BEETLE, STANDARD, CRYSTAL, BOX ELDER, TIGER, #12–#18

PARACHUTE HOPPER, #6–#12

CRICKET, #10–#12

STREAMERS

MUDDLER MINNOW AND WOOLHEAD SCULPIN, #6–#10

Gardner River (Map 3)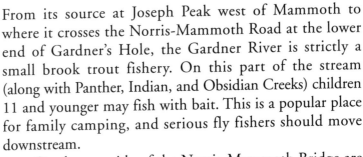

CUTTHROAT • BROOK TROUT • BROWN TROUT • RAINBOW TROUT • MOUNTAIN WHITEFISH

From its source at Joseph Peak west of Mammoth to where it crosses the Norris-Mammoth Road at the lower end of Gardner's Hole, the Gardner River is strictly a small brook trout fishery. On this part of the stream (along with Panther, Indian, and Obsidian Creeks) children 11 and younger may fish with bait. This is a popular place for family camping, and serious fly fishers should move downstream.

On the east side of the Norris-Mammoth Bridge are Sheepeater Cliffs, and there's good fishing for 8- to 10-inch brook trout here. Below Sheepeater Cliffs, the river drops 150 feet over Osprey Falls into 800-foot-deep Sheepeater Canyon. The river in this area is practically fishless, and getting into and out of this canyon is dangerous. The river becomes fishable again about 1½ miles below Osprey Falls. The only access to this section is at the Tower Bridge, via the Mammoth-Tower Road. Only ½ mile of fishable water lies upstream of the bridge before the hazards of hiking begin to outweigh the rewards of catching a few pan-sized trout.

Downstream from the Mammoth-Tower Bridge the river flows through Gardner Canyon, a pleasant 3-mile hike along sagebrush and greasewood trails. Lava Creek enters from the east, adding nutrients and a few cutthroat trout to the river, which they share with brooks, browns, rainbows,

Gardner River

and a few large whitefish. Most of the stream is typical canyon water, with boulders, riffles, and runs. There are also a few nice pools in this stretch. The middle of this short canyon is accessible via a trail behind the Yellowstone School and Mammoth housing area.

The 45th Parallel Bridge—so called because it's halfway between the equator and the North Pole—crosses the Gardner River at the bottom of the canyon. From here to the north boundary of the Park, the river plunges through 3 miles of cascades and boulders, known locally as Shotgun Chutes, before entering the Yellowstone River at the town of Gardiner, Montana. Although the river flows alongside the road and access is easy, the character of the water makes fishing difficult.

From the Mammoth-Tower Bridge to the Park boundary, searching the water with attractor dries, nymphs, and streamers will be most productive. The only hatches you need concern yourself with are the Salmonfly and Golden Stonefly emergences. During terrestrial time, July through

September, grasshoppers, beetles, and gargantuan Mormon Cricket patterns will bring trout to the surface. The average resident trout here run 10 to 12 inches, but an occasional lunker brown will make you wish you'd put on fresh backing this season.

Autumn is a colorful time on the Gardner. Aspen leaves are turning red and gold, bull elk are bugling and sparring for their harems, and big brown trout begin migrating up the Gardner from the Yellowstone River. While the fishing in September is okay, October is the best time to try for fall-migrating fish. Rainy or snowy days are best for fishing big streamers, nymphs, and *Baetis* mayfly imitations to fall-run browns. Even on bright, sunny days, the Gardner is one of those rare rivers where you can still get into migratory fish with big attractor dries and terrestrials. Regardless of the weather, we always make it a point to fish the Gardner every fall.

SELECTED EMERGENCES

MAYFLIES

SPECIES	MAY	JUNE	JULY	AUG.	SEPT.	OCT.
BAETIS					■■■	■■■

CADDIS

SPECIES	MAY	JUNE	JULY	AUG.	SEPT.	OCT.
VARIOUS SPECIES; none predominates			■■■	■■■		

STONEFLIES

SPECIES	MAY	JUNE	JULY	AUG.	SEPT.	OCT.
SALMONFLY		■■■				
GOLDEN STONEFLY			■■■			
LITTLE YELLOW STONE			■■■	■■		

TERRESTRIALS

SPECIES	MAY	JUNE	JULY	AUG.	SEPT.	OCT.
ANTS, BEETLES, CRICKETS, AND GRASSHOPPERS			■■■	■■■	■■■	■■■

SELECTED FLY PATTERNS

MAYFLIES

BAETIS

PHEASANT TAIL NYMPH, #18–#20

BAETIS SPARKLE DUN, #18–#20

CADDISFLIES

GREEN CADDIS LARVA, #12–#14

X-CADDIS, #14–#18

ELK HAIR CADDIS, TAN, #12–#18

STONEFLIES

BROOKS' BLACK STONE NYMPH, #6–#10

KAUFMANN'S BLACK SEAL STONE NYMPH, #6–#10

NICK'S GOLDEN STONE NYMPH, #6–#10

KAUFMANN'S AMBER SEAL STONE NYMPH, #6–#10

IMPROVED SOFA PILLOW, #4–#6

KAUFMANN'S YELLOW STIMULATOR, #6–#16

Stonefly nymphs
(Clockwise from left)
Nick's Salmonfly,
Kaufmann's Seal Stone,
Brooks' Stone

ATTRACTORS

PRINCE NYMPH, #6–#16

SERENDIPITY, LIME AND RED, #14–#16

FLASHBACK HARE'S EAR, #10–#16

ROYAL STIMULATOR, #12–#16

GOOFUS BUG, #12–#18

ADAMS, #14–#18

H&L VARIANT, #12–#16

TERRESTRIALS

YELLOWSTONE FLYING ANT, #12–#16

FOAM BEETLE STANDARD, CRYSTAL, #12–#16

DAVE'S AND PARACHUTE HOPPERS, #8–#14

SLOUGH CREEK CRICKET, #6–#8

STREAMERS

CRYSTAL BUGGER, BROWN AND OLIVE, #6

WOOLHEAD SCULPIN, BLACK AND OLIVE, #6

LIGHT SPRUCE, #4–#6

Gibbon River (Map 4)

BROOK TROUT • BROWN TROUT • RAINBOW TROUT • GRAYLING • MOUNTAIN WHITEFISH

The Gibbon River has it all: meandering meadow stretches with deep undercuts inhabited by big browns, riffles with rambunctious rainbows, pockets holding voracious brook trout, and secluded pools hiding the elusive grayling.

After leaving its main sources, Grebe and Wolf Lakes, the Gibbon flows through a maze of downed lodgepole pines until crossing the Norris-Canyon Road on its way to Virginia Meadows. This section of stream is best left to its resident moose and bear, as human travel is next to impossible amid the downed timber.

Virginia Meadows begins on the downstream side of the Norris-Canyon Highway and offers fine fishing for

Gibbon River

small brook trout. There's a picnic area at the lower end of the meadow, accessible via the Virginia Cascades Road. The entrance to this one-way drive is about 2 miles downstream from the meadow and follows the river back upstream to both the cascades and the picnic area. Below the cascades and for the 2 miles downstream to Norris Junction, the water is full of pockets, pools, and undercut banks that hold plenty of browns, brooks, rainbows, and the occasional grayling. It's best fished with a high-floating dry fly bounced over and through the scattered cover that lines the stream.

At Norris Junction, with the addition of water from Solfatara Creek, the river changes its character, becoming noticeably deeper and wider as it passes the campground and crosses the Norris-Gardiner Road. From here to Elk Park, a distance of about 2 miles, the river flows behind Norris Geyser Basin; the browns become larger, the brook trout fewer, and the rainbows far between. Geothermal features start to appear along the stream, adding both nutrients and water and preparing the habitat for increased insect life as the river turns the corner into Elk Park.

If you head south at Norris Junction, Elk Park will be the first meadow on your right and a great place to see elk. The river is like a spring creek here, with slow-moving water and tremendously undercut banks. The insect hatches also resemble those of a spring creek: *Baetis* (Blue-Winged Olives), Pale Morning Duns, Brown Drakes, and Green Drakes. Caddis include *Oecetis* and *Lepidostoma.* This is on-your-knees fishing to wary brown trout. Sharply honed stalking skills and a high degree of patience are required to land fish here. You must be able to focus and concentrate. The only time we recommend searching the water with a fly is during terrestrial season.

As you journey downstream from Elk Park the elevation drops radically, and there's a mile of unproductive, shallow rapids next to the road. The gradient then levels and the water slows at the Gibbon picnic area, upstream of Gibbon Meadows.

The scene here is much the same as at Elk Park, only this meadow is much larger. The depth is also more uniform, and the flow more even, in this stretch. There are fewer undercut banks and weed beds, and it isn't as obvious where trout hold. If you don't spot any surface feeding, look for fish holding in the shadows next to the bank. Like Elk Park, Gibbon Meadows can be difficult fishing, but it's a lot of fun for someone who enjoys mixing hunting with fishing.

Leaving Gibbon Meadows behind, the river becomes pocket water all the way down to Gibbon Falls, a distance of 5 miles. This is fun fishing for anyone who likes searching the water with attractor flies for 8- to 12-inch fish. Browns and rainbows predominate in this, the Gibbon River Canyon, along with the occasional grayling and small brook trout.

At Gibbon Falls the water drops 88 feet, forming a barrier to migrating trout. The river here is a succession of riffles, runs, and pools, custom made for the wet-fly and nymph angler. It's good fishing during June's Golden Stonefly emergence and a favorite with many locals during grasshopper time. However, this section is especially noted for its fine fall fishing.

In October, from Gibbon Falls 5 miles downstream to the river's confluence with the Firehole at Madison Junction, large brown and rainbow trout head into the river to spawn. These fall-run fish, moving upstream from Montana's Hebgen Lake, attract fishers from around the world.

SELECTED EMERGENCES

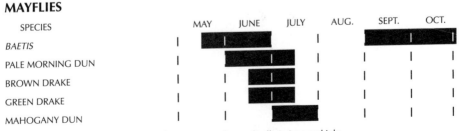

MAYFLIES

SPECIES	MAY	JUNE	JULY	AUG.	SEPT.	OCT.
BAETIS						
PALE MORNING DUN						
BROWN DRAKE						
GREEN DRAKE						
MAHOGANY DUN						

Green Drakes and Mahogany Duns may be encountered sporadically in June and July.

CADDIS

SPECIES	MAY	JUNE	JULY	AUG.	SEPT.	OCT.
LEPIDOSTOMA		██████	██████			
OECETIS		██████	██████			

STONEFLIES

SPECIES	MAY	JUNE	JULY	AUG.	SEPT.	OCT.
GOLDEN STONEFLY		███				
LITTLE YELLOW STONE		███████	██████			

TERRESTRIALS

SPECIES	MAY	JUNE	JULY	AUG.	SEPT.	OCT.
ANTS, BEETLES, CRICKETS, AND GRASSHOPPERS			████████	████████	████████	██

SELECTED FLY PATTERNS

MAYFLIES

BAETIS

PHEASANT TAIL NYMPH, #18–#22

BAETIS SOFT HACKLE EMERGER, #20–#22

BAETIS SPARKLE DUN, #18–#22

BAETIS BIPLANE, #20–#22

PALE MORNING DUN (PMD)

PMD NYMPH, #16–#18

PMD EMERGER, #16–#18

PMD SPARKLE DUN, #16–#18

PMD SPINNER, #16

BROWN DRAKE

BROWN DRAKE EMERGER, SPARKLE DUN, AND SPINNER, #8–#12

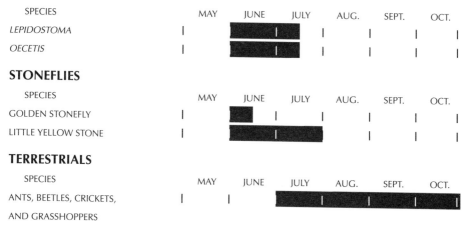

Baetis Dun

CADDIS

X-CADDIS, GREEN AND OLIVE, #16–#18

GODDARD CADDIS, #16

STONEFLIES

NICK'S GOLDEN STONE NYMPH, #6–#8

KAUFMANN'S GOLDEN STONE NYMPH, #6–#8

LIGHT HARE'S EAR NYMPH, #12–#14 (FOR LITTLE YELLOW STONE)

KAUFMANN'S YELLOW STIMULATOR, #6–#16

    (FOR BOTH GOLDEN STONEFLY AND LITTLE YELLOW STONE ADULTS)

ATTRACTORS

YELLOW GOOFUS, #12–#16

H&L VARIANT, #12=#16

ROYAL WULFF, #12–#16

TERRESTRIALS

FOAM OR FUR ANT, BLACK, #16–#18

FOAM BEETLE, #12–#16 (EFFECTIVE IN THE MEADOWS)

DAVE'S AND PARACHUTE HOPPERS, #10–#14

(HOPPER PATTERNS MUST RIDE LOW IN THE WATER)

STREAMERS

LIGHT SPRUCE, #4–#6

FALL SOFT HACKLES, WHITE, YELLOW, OLIVE AND BLACK, #6

Glen Creek (Map 3)

BROOK TROUT

 This small meadow stream is fun to fish for cubby little brook trout that average 8 inches. It's located near the Bunsen Peak Loop Road about 5 miles south of Mammoth, on the Mammoth-Tower Highway. The backdrop for this stream is the beautiful Gardner's Hole, a place once famous for its mountain-man rendezvous during the early 1800s. This is a good place for beginners to catch that first Yellowstone trout.

Gneiss Creek (Map 1)

BROOK TROUT • BROWN TROUT • RAINBOW TROUT

 This small, swampy, meadow stream is one of the tributaries that form Duck Creek. The Gneiss Creek Trail begins at the Fir Ridge Cemetery, 9 miles north of West Yellowstone on Highway 191. By the time you take the 4-mile hike from the cemetery to the stream, you're in the middle of prime grizzly bear and moose territory. There are better, safer, and easier places to catch 10-inch trout than here.

Grayling Creek (Map 1)

BROWN TROUT • CUTTHROAT • RAINBOW TROUT

This creek follows Highway 191 north of West Yellowstone, from Mile Marker 11 upstream to Mile Marker 17. Most of the fishing takes place along this stretch, because Grayling's headwater contains small fish and is located in trailless backcountry that's often closed to human travel due to high grizzly bear activity.

Grayling Creek is a medium-sized mountain stream that offers excellent fishing during hatches. Green Drakes and Pale Morning Duns (including PMD spinner falls), caddis, and Little Yellow and Golden Stoneflies will bring the trout to the surface. Brown, cutthroat, and rainbow trout average 11 inches, but those anglers willing to hunt will find an occasional lunker.

Grayling Creek

Indian Creek (Map 3)

BROOK TROUT

This large tributary to the Gardner River is located 8½ miles south of Mammoth, on the Mammoth-Norris Highway at the Indian Creek campground. Anglers can expect to catch plenty of brook trout averaging 6 inches. This stream receives a lot of fishing pressure due to its proximity to a campground and its special regulations, which allow children 11 years and younger to fish with worms. This stream is a good place to bring beginning anglers. They *will* catch trout.

Landslide Creek (Map 3)

BROWN TROUT • CUTTHROAT

Located about 1½ miles west of Gardiner, Montana, on the old Gardiner-Cinnabar Road, this little tributary to the Yellowstone River contains small cutthroat and brown trout averaging 7 inches in a good year.

Lava Creek (Map 3)

BROOK TROUT • RAINBOW TROUT

Lava Creek is a small tributary that enters the Gardner River about 2 miles east of Mammoth, below the Mammoth-Tower Bridge. The lower stream runs through a canyon all the way upstream to Undine Falls, a distance of nearly 4 miles, and offers poor fishing for small brook and rainbow trout. Brown trout may run up from the main river sporadically. Above the falls and the Lava Creek picnic area, the fishing is good for brook trout running up to 9 or 10 inches. There's no trail up the creek, and this area was heavily burned during the 1988 fires, making navigation a chore. But it's a fun stream to fish, where dapping is a preferred technique.

Lupine Creek (Map 3)

BROOK TROUT

 This tiny tributary to Lava Creek contains a sparse population of brook trout, not worth pursuing.

Madison River (Map 1)

BROWN TROUT • RAINBOW TROUT • MOUNTAIN WHITEFISH

National Park Mountain overlooks the beginning of the Madison River, which is formed by the confluence of the Gibbon and Firehole Rivers. It was here that a small group of men with foresight conceived the idea of setting aside the natural wonders of Yellowstone as a national park.

The Madison River has been called the world's largest chalkstream. From Madison Junction to the west entrance

Madison River

of the Park is a 14-mile journey. The road follows the river for 10 of these miles, making access easy. The fishing, however, is never easy. According to Charlie Brooks, in his *Trout and the Stream* (Crown, New York, 1974), only 20 percent of those fishing this water catch fish. Success demands a stealthy approach and all the concentration you can muster.

From Elk Meadow downstream to Big Bend, then past Mount Haynes and Nine-Mile Hole to Riverside Drive, the river is a succession of deep runs with undercut banks. The bottom is randomly carpeted with lush weeds that reach the surface, creating a complex mix of crosscurrents. Controlling drag is paramount to fishing this stretch successfully. We advise long leaders and tippets to help achieve drag-free floats.

This 9-mile chalkstream section is home to several important trout stream insects. Mayflies include *Baetis* (BWOs), Pale Morning Duns, Gray Drakes, and Tricos. While several caddis are available to the trout, we've found only *Brachycentrus* adults present in sufficient number to entertain rising fish. Salmonflies are the predominant stonefly and therefore the stonefly of choice. This early-June hatch is extremely variable, confined to short sections of riffle water where the habitat is ideal for the nymphs.

From July through September, terrestrials form an increasing portion of the trout diet. Good places to fish imitations are the meadow stretches of Elk Meadow to Big Bend, then downstream to the bottom reaches of this section, most notably Grasshopper Bank. At Riverside Drive, just below Grasshopper Bank, the river loses its chalkstream character and becomes freestone-riffle water.

The next 5 miles of river, from Riverside Drive to the Barns' Pools, lacks holding water and is mostly unproductive. With the exception of a few very short runs such as Shakey Beiley's, the river in this section is not worth your time. It's just too shallow.

A half mile inside Yellowstone's West Entrance is a dirt road on the north side of the main road that takes you down to the Barns Pools, named for the stables that used to house the Park's horses and stagecoaches. When you reach the end of the road, you'll be at Hole #1. Around the corner upstream is Cable Car Run, and around the corner downstream are two more holes, locally named, with great imagination, Hole #2 and Hole #3. For the next 3 miles downstream, the river winds northwest in a series of oxbows to the Park's boundary. This portion of the river is only accessible by hiking downstream from the Barns' Pools or upstream from the Baker's Hole campground and the Montana state line.

Many refer to this part of the river as Beaver Meadows, because of the numerous beaver holes along the banks. This area is a haven for moose and bears, which like the security of the willows and bogs and nearby thick stands of lodgepole pines. As the river meanders through this meadow, deep pools and enormous undercut banks provide great holding water and security for trout and whitefish. This stretch is primarily a fall fishery, hosting great numbers of migrating trout that move upstream from Montana's Hebgen Lake to spawn. A resident population of trout is virtually nonexistent.

Late September through October is the time to fish the fall spawners in the Madison. Short days, cold weather, and snow squalls signal both the fish and a hearty breed of fishers that it's time to return to the Madison. Heavy rods, large tippets, and big flies are required to land these lake fish moving in to spawn. Fish of up to 4 pounds are not uncommon.

For gear we recommend a 7-weight rod, 1X–2X tippets, and a good selection of big nymphs and streamers in various colors. This type of fishing is not unlike steelhead and salmon fishing. These fish are territorial, protecting their turf rather than actively feeding. We believe in using big, bright flies to take advantage of this aggressiveness.

Although we look forward to the fall fishing each year, it marks the beginning of the end. November means big snows, bitter cold, and the close of the season.

SELECTED EMERGENCES

MAYFLIES

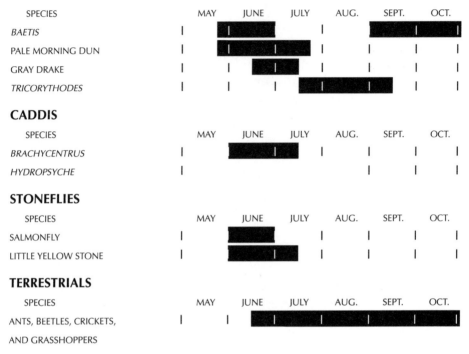

SPECIES	MAY	JUNE	JULY	AUG.	SEPT.	OCT.
BAETIS						
PALE MORNING DUN						
GRAY DRAKE						
TRICORYTHODES						

CADDIS

SPECIES	MAY	JUNE	JULY	AUG.	SEPT.	OCT.
BRACHYCENTRUS						
HYDROPSYCHE						

STONEFLIES

SPECIES	MAY	JUNE	JULY	AUG.	SEPT.	OCT.
SALMONFLY						
LITTLE YELLOW STONE						

TERRESTRIALS

SPECIES	MAY	JUNE	JULY	AUG.	SEPT.	OCT.
ANTS, BEETLES, CRICKETS, AND GRASSHOPPERS						

SELECTED FLY PATTERNS

MAYFLIES

BAETIS

PHEASANT TAIL NYMPH, #18–#22

BAETIS SOFT HACKLE EMERGER, #20–#22

BAETIS SPARKLE DUN, #18–#22

BAETIS BIPLANE (CRIPPLE), #20–#22

PALE MORNING DUN (PMD)

PMD NYMPH, #16

PMD EMERGER, #16–#18

PMD SPARKLE DUN, #16–#18

PMD SPINNER, #16–#18

GRAY DRAKE

GRAY DRAKE SPARKLE DUN, PARADRAKE, AND SPINNER, #10–#12

TRICORYTHODES

TRICO SPARKLE DUN AND NO HACKLE, #20–#22

TRICO SPINNER, #20–#22

CADDIS

BRACHYCENTRUS

    PEACOCK & STARLING, #16

    ANTRON CADDIS PUPA, OLIVE, #16

    X-CADDIS, OLIVE, #16

    HENRYVILLE OR HEMINGWAY CADDIS, #14–#16

HYDROPSYCHE

    ANTRON CADDIS PUPA, BROWN, #16

    IRISE HYDROPSYCHE, #17 (TIEMCO 102Y)

    X-CADDIS, TAN, #16

    SPENT CADDIS, TAN, #16

Brachycentrus pupa

STONEFLIES

SALMONFLY

    BROOKS' BLACK STONE NYMPH, #4–#8

    KAUFMANN'S BLACK SEAL STONE, #4–#8

    HENRY'S FORK SALMONFLY, #4–#6

LITTLE YELLOW STONE

    LITTLE YELLOW STONEFLY NYMPH, #10–#14

    KAUFMANN STIMULATOR, YELLOW, #10–#16

STREAMERS

    FLY FUR STREAMER, RAINBOW, BROWN, WHITEFISH, #6

    WOOLLY BUGGER, BLACK, OLIVE, YELLOW, #2–#6

    BAKER'S HOLE BUGGER, #4–#8

TERRESTRIALS

    FOAM ANT, #14–#20

    FOAM BEETLE, #12–#18

    JOE'S AND DAVE'S HOPPERS, #8–#12

Maple Creek (Map 1)

BROOK TROUT • BROWN TROUT

This tiny tributary to Cougar Creek is crossed by the Gneiss Creek Trail halfway between its beginning and its end, right in the middle of heavy grizzly country. It isn't worth the hike or the fishing for tiny brook and brown trout averaging 5 inches.

Mol Heron Creek (Map 2)

CUTTHROAT

This small stream leaves Sportsman Lake on the northern boundary of the Park and contains cutthroat trout averaging 8 to 9 inches. It can be reached by an 11-mile hike east up the Specimen Creek Trail; the trailhead is on Highway 191, Mile Marker 27, north of West Yellowstone. You can also get there by hiking 13 miles west from Mammoth on the Sportsman Lake Trail, but it isn't worth the hike whichever trail you choose.

Obsidian Creek (Map 3)

BROOK TROUT

This small tributary flows into the Gardner River near the Indian Creek campground, about 7 miles south of Mammoth. It's a fine little brook trout stream, with fish averaging 7 inches, and it's one of four streams with special regulations that allow children 11 years of age and under to fish with worms. It's a given that the kids will catch trout, and there's a good chance you'll see moose browsing the willows along the stream. Be sure to stop nearby at Apollinaris Spring for a drink of its naturally effervescent water.

Oxbow Creek (Map 3)

BROOK TROUT

Oxbow Creek is a small, freestone tributary to the Yellowstone River, located near the middle of the Black Canyon of the Yellowstone. There's no trail along the stream, and it's essentially fishless, except for a small population of tiny brook trout found near its confluence with the Yellowstone River.

Panther Creek (Map 3)

BROOK TROUT

Another of the specially regulated streams that allow children 11 years of age and younger to fish with worms,

Panther Creek is a small tributary to the Gardner River, easily reached via the Bighorn Pass Trail near the Indian Creek campground, 8½ miles south of Mammoth on the Mammoth-Norris Road. Seven-inch brook trout are the average, and highly visible flies such as Wulffs, Trudes, and grasshoppers are all you need to catch them.

Reese Creek (Map 3)

BROWN TROUT • CUTTHROAT

Named for George "Tough" Reese, a placer miner who owned a ranch at the mouth of the stream in the 1860s, Reese Creek is a tributary to the Yellowstone River, with a small population of peewee cutthroat and brown trout, located just west of the North Entrance to the Park. Take the Gardiner-Cinnabar Road west from Gardiner, Montana, for about 5 miles. Reese Creek doesn't see much fishing pressure, for obvious reasons.

Richards Creek (Map 1)

This small creek drains Richards Pond and enters Duck Creek 1 mile east of the Park boundary, 8 miles north of West Yellowstone, off Highway 191. Richards Creek holds only a few trout fry less than 2 inches long.

Secret Valley Creek (Map 4)

BROOK TROUT

This tiny creek is hard to find, hence its name. Located ¼ mile upstream from Gibbon Falls, on the Madison Junction-Norris Highway, this little tributary to the Gibbon River flows through a marsh and holds a sparse population of 4- to 5-inch brook trout, mainly in the lower sections. Secret Valley itself is a lovely hike, if trout fishing isn't in your plans. Keep to the hillside along the valley, because the valley floor is too marshy for walking.

Snowslide Creek (Map 2)

This tiny tributary to the Gallatin River, located on the west side of Highway 191 at Mile Marker 25, north of West Yellowstone, appears to be fishless.

Solfatara Creek (Map 4)

BROOK TROUT • BROWN TROUT • RAINBOW TROUT • GRAYLING

Solfatara Creek enters the Gibbon River at Norris Junction, near the ranger station. The crowds of campers at the Norris campground make fly fishing difficult. But if you fish it when their numbers diminish here, you can do surprisingly well; it's inhabited by brown, brook, and rainbow trout, and at times grayling. Hatches on the Gibbon often spill over into its smaller tributaries—Gray and Brown Drakes, PMDs, and a few caddis species—and when this happens, Solfatara Creek can provide excellent fishing for trout that average 9 inches.

Specimen Creek (Map 2

CUTHROAT • RAINBOW TROUT

This lovely little tributary to the Gallatin River is located at Mile Marker 27 on Highway 191 north of West Yellowstone. The main stream divides into the North and East Forks 2 miles upstream from the Specimen Creek trailhead. The fishing is best from its confluence with the Gallatin upstream to the forks; you'll find resident rainbow-cutthroat hybrids averaging 9 inches. The East Fork is surrounded by dense overgrowth and downfalls, which make fly fishing difficult. The North Fork offers a little more room to maneuver, but the fish in both forks are sparse and small.

Stellaria Creek (Map 2)

This tributary to the east fork of Fan Creek appears to be fishless.

Stephens Creek (Map 3)

BROWN TROUT • CUTTHROAT

This small tributary to the Yellowstone River, located about 2 miles west of Gardiner, Montana, on the old Gardiner-Cinnabar Road, contains small populations of cutthroat and brown trout.

Straight Creek (Map 3)

BROOK TROUT

This fine little brook-trout fishery flows both into and out of Grizzly Lake. It's located along the Grizzly Lake Trail, about 6 miles north of Norris Junction on the Mammoth-Norris Road. Above the lake, Straight Creek provides little habitat for trout; below the lake, it merges with Winter Creek and supports a good population of wild brook trout averaging 8 inches. In July there's a hatch of Green Drakes, providing fun dry-fly fishing for eager brookies.

Tower Creek

Tower Creek (Map 3)

BROOK TROUT • RAINBOW TROUT

This rough-and-tumble, medium-sized trout stream enters the Yellowstone River near the Tower Falls campground. Upstream from the campground, Tower Creek offers excellent fishing for 9-inch brook and rainbow trout; the Tower Creek Trail parallels it. Below the campground, a well-traveled trail takes you down to the Yellowstone River, where you can fish your way upstream to the spectacular Tower Falls itself. The lower water, from the Yellowstone River to Tower Falls, is best fished with high-floating attractor flies such as Trudes, Wulffs, and H&L Variants. Above the falls, upstream from the campground during July, August, and September, try terrestrials such as beetles and grasshoppers.

Winter Creek (Map 3)

BROOK TROUT

This small tributary to Straight Creek, located off the Mount Holmes Trail, has a population of brook trout, but they are considerably smaller and fewer in number than in neighboring Straight Creek.

LAKES AND PONDS

Beaver Lake (Map 3)

Technically, this mosquito-laden 22-acre mudflat holds small brook trout. Located 7½ miles north of Norris Junction, on the west side of the Mammoth–Norris Highway, Beaver Lake, formed by a beaver dam on Obsidian Creek, originally had good fishing. Now it has silted in, and it's no longer much of a lake—or a fishery.

Blacktail Pond (Map 3)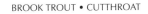

BROOK TROUT • CUTTHROAT

This 11-acre pond lies surrounded by sagebrush about 150 yards off the Mammoth–Tower Highway, 7 miles east of Mammoth. The pond is surrounded by bogs and marshy grasses, and you can get into trouble if you don't pay attention. It's not unusual to catch cutthroat and brook trout 14 inches or larger, and the fish are always healthy and saturated with color. *Callibaetis* mayflies and damselfly hatches will bring the large resident fish to the surface. If there are no hatches, you'll have to go with nymphs. We recommend damselflies, dragonflies, scuds, Zug Bugs, and Hare's Ears.

Cache Lake

Fishless.

Cascade Lake (Map 4)

CUTTHROAT • GRAYLING

Cascade Lake contains cutthroat trout averaging 12 inches and grayling averaging 9 inches. It's accessible via the Howard Eaton Trail, ½ mile west of Canyon Junction on the Norris-Canyon Highway; or via the Cascade Lake Picnic Area Trail, 11¼ miles north of Canyon Junction on the Canyon–Tower Highway. There's a lot of bear activity in this area.

Crag Lake

Fishless.

Crescent Lake

Fishless.

Divide Lake

Like Crag and Crescent Lakes, Divide Lake is fishless; in low-water years it dries up by August. It's adjacent to Highway 191, 19 miles north of West Yellowstone, and on summer weekends you may see a local prankster toting a stuffed 20-pound lake trout to his car. This brings traffic to a halt and rods out of the trunk, but trust us: There are no fish in this lake.

Fawn Lake (Map 3)

BROOK TROUT

You can reach this five-acre brook trout lake from the Glen Creek Trailhead, 5 miles south of Mammoth, near the Golden Gate. Take the Glen Creek Trail until it intersects with the Fawn Pass Trail, then continue on to the lake, a distance of about 5 miles and about a two-hour hike. This trail is infamous for grizzly bears; it's not uncommon to see two or three bears on the way to the lake. Undertake this hike only in groups of four or more, and carry pepper spray as a precaution. The shores of the lake are marshy, and it's difficult to maneuver into position to cast to the brook trout, which average 12 inches.

Floating Island Lake

Fishless.

Gallatin Lake

Fishless.

Geode Lake

Fishless.

Grebe Lake

Grebe Lake (Map 4)

RAINBOW TROUT • GRAYLING

This 156-acre lake supports a good population of rainbow trout and grayling that average 14 and 11 inches, respectively. It's best reached by a 3-mile hike from the Grebe Lake Trailhead, found 3½ miles west of Canyon Junction, on the Norris-Canyon Highway. Although you can fish the lake from shore, we advise using a float tube, because the fish always seem to be just out of casting range.

If you want to catch a grayling, this is the place to do it—one of the few places left in the lower 48 states with a natural population. The 3-mile, level hike to the lake is worth the effort. At ice-out (mid-June), grayling congregate in the lake's outlet to spawn. By midseason they've moved in among the lily pads and weed beds to feed on emerging *Callibaetis* and damselflies. In late August the lake fishes well with grasshopper and ant patterns.

Grizzly Lake (Map 3)

BROOK TROUT

This long, narrow, 136-acre lake holds brook trout that average 8 inches. It's located 6 miles north of Norris Junction, on the west side of the Mammoth-Norris Highway. There are two ways to get to it. The shorter and more difficult is over the Grizzly Lake Trail, a 2-mile hike of switchbacks that take you up and across a ridge and down to the lake. The longer and easier route is along Straight Creek, which offers good fishing all the way upstream to the lake. The larger brookies here prefer a moving fly; a size-14 Adams animated with 6- to 10-inch strips will elicit vicious takes.

Harlequin Lake

Fishless, but a nice hike.

High Lake (Map 2)

CUTTHROAT

This pretty, seven-acre lake is the headwater of the East Fork of Specimen Creek. Appropriately named for its elevation of 8,774 feet, High Lake is best reached by the Specimen Creek Trail, located 27 miles north of West Yellowstone on Highway 191. This seldom-visited lake lies on the north boundary of the Park, and it's a long hike (9 miles) for the cutthroat, which average 9 to 10 inches.

Ice Lake (Map 4)

RAINBOW TROUT

This 224-acre lake is near Wolf Lake, and is reached by an easy, ¼-mile hike over the Ice Lake Trail. Most people consider the lake fishless, but there are reports of a few large fish remaining from previous plantings.

Joffe Lake (Map 3)

BROOK TROUT

Only one and a half acres, this old reservoir is 2 miles south of Mammoth. To get there, take the dirt road that heads south off the Mammoth-Norris Highway, a little over a mile south of Mammoth. Stay to the right and you'll come to the lake in about a mile. The resident brook trout, which average 7 inches, always seem to be rising here. This is a good place to bring beginning fly fishers; they'll catch rising trout.

Lost Lake

Fishless.

Lake of the Woods

Fishless.

Nymph Lake

Fishless.

Obsidian Lake

Fishless.

Phantom Lake

Fishless.

Rainbow Lakes

Fishless.

Richards Pond (Map 1)

BROOK TROUT

Years ago this pond was formed by a beaver dam that backed up the springs in the area. Originally it had good fishing for brook trout, but the beavers moved out in 1987, and the fires swept through here in 1988. Since then the pond has filled with silt and no longer has habitat for trout. This area is often closed because of grizzly bears.

Shelf Lake

Fishless.

Slide Lakes (Map 3)

RAINBOW TROUT

To reach these two lakes, take the one-way Old Gardiner Road, behind the Mammoth Hot Spring Hotel. Head north for about 1¾ miles and you'll see the barren Big Slide Lake on your left. Little Slide Lake is directly below it and contains a small population of rainbow trout. Both of these lakes were formed by beaver dams and mud slides, and this provides poor spawning habitat for the resident trout. Viewing the wildlife in this area is usually more entertaining than the fishing. Antelope, bears, deer, coyotes, and elk are often seen here.

Sportsman Lake (Map 2)

CUTTHROAT

This four-acre lake is nestled in the Gallatin Range near the Park's north boundary, more or less halfway between the trailheads for the 11-mile-long Specimen Creek and the 13-mile-long Sportsman Lake Trails. The Specimen Creek Trailhead is 27 miles north of West Yellowstone on Highway 191, while the Sportsman Lake Trail is accessible from a number of points near Mammoth. The hike is beautiful and the fishing is good for 10-inch cutthroats, but the distance definitely makes this an overnight proposition.

Swan Lake

Fishless.

Trilobite Lake (Map 3)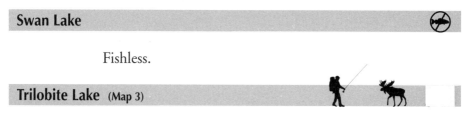

BROOK TROUT

Unnamed on many maps, this 11-acre lake is wedged into the Gallatin Range between Mount Holmes and Dome Mountain; its elevation is 8,366 feet, and it holds foot-long brook trout. The lake is reached by a 9-mile hike over the Winter Creek Trail, which starts at Apollinaris Spring, 9½ miles north of Norris Junction, on the Mammoth-Norris Highway. The last 3 miles to the lake are along an unmaintained trail, and this area has a lot of grizzly bear activity. Seriously consider this before making the trek.

Twin Lakes—North and South

Fishless.

Wolf Lake (Map 4)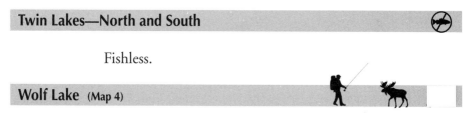

RAINBOW TROUT • GRAYLING

This 51-acre lake is best reached by either of two trails along the Norris-Canyon Highway. The first, a 4-mile hike, departs from the Ice Lake Trailhead found about 3½ miles east of Norris Junction. The second is the Grebe Lake Trail, a 5-mile hike found about 3½ miles west of Canyon Junction. The lake contains good populations of rainbow trout and grayling that average 10 inches.

2

NORTHEAST

LAMAR AND YELLOWSTONE RIVERS
AND THE CANYON

Arguably the most beautiful area of the Park, the northeast quadrant contains three of the most popular streams—the Lamar and Yellowstone Rivers, and Slough Creek—all home to the native Yellowstone cutthroat trout.

The Lamar River is a late bloomer, usually the last river in the Park to clear of snowmelt. But when it comes on, it comes on strong, with good fishing using grasshoppers and other terrestrials in late July. This situation reverses that on most other rivers in the Park—where hatches come early in the season and terrestrials follow. Tributaries of the Lamar, Slough Creek, and Soda Butte Creek are also popular with anglers, who make it a yearly ritual to fish each stream.

The Yellowstone River is the world's finest trout stream. Through far-sighted fisheries management, its cutthroats are more numerous and larger than they were 30 years ago. Downstream from Yellowstone Lake and

The Yellowstone River leaving Yellowstone Lake

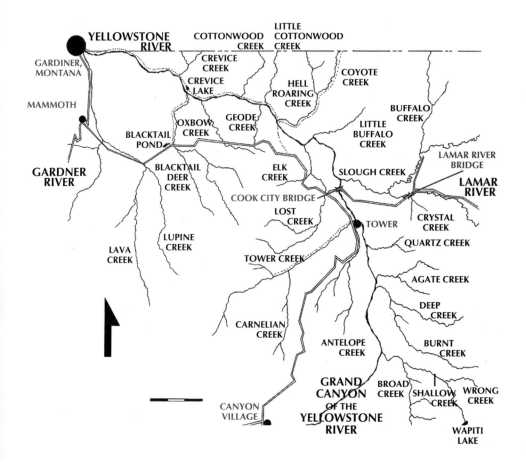

Map 5 — The Canyon

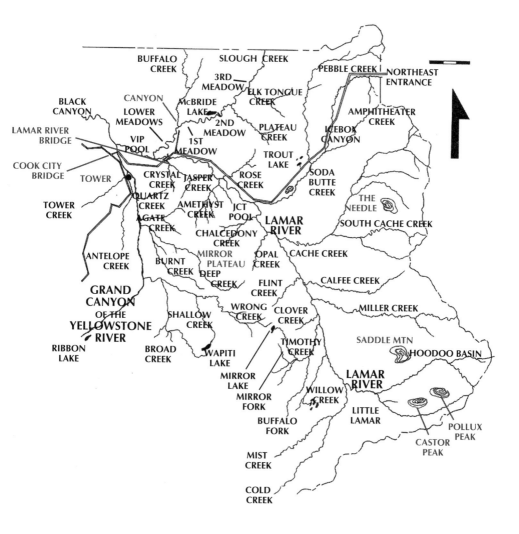

Map 6 — Lamar River

Map 7 — Yellowstone River

above the falls, the Yellowstone is an insect factory. We've counted hatches of at least 11 major mayflies, six caddis, and two stoneflies that are important to the trout diet. At times, the number of different species of flies on the water can be overwhelming. Native cutthroats have the reputation of being easy to catch, but on this part of the Yellowstone the cutthroats can be more selective than a spring-creek brown.

From its Grand Canyon downstream to the town of Gardiner, Montana, the Yellowstone and its tributaries are a long way from the road. The trout here see less pressure and are more cooperative. Bring your pack, camera, and bear bells, and have a good time.

RIVERS AND STREAMS

Agate Creek (Map 5)

BROWN TROUT • CUTTHROAT • RAINBOW TROUT

You reach Agate Creek by taking the Specimen Ridge Trail south from the trailhead, about ½ mile east of the Cooke City Bridge. Take the trail 3 miles to the Agate Creek Trail, then follow this trail 3 miles to the confluence of the creek with the Yellowstone River. The lower reaches contain small populations of brown, cutthroat, and rainbow trout. Agate Creek is a nursery and the fish are small, but you can catch a better one now and then if the fish run in from the Yellowstone.

Alum Creek (Map 7)

CUTTHROAT

Crossed by the Canyon–Fishing Bridge Highway in Hayden Valley, Alum Creek is a spawning stream for Yellowstone cutthroats. It's closed to angling.

Amethyst Creek

Fishless.

Amphitheater Creek (Map 6)

CUTTHROAT

This small tributary enters Soda Butte Creek from the east, on the east side of the road, just downstream of Icebox Canyon. Be sure to take a look at Icebox Canyon, a frigid corridor that retains its massive chunks of ice throughout the year. The Thunderer Cutoff Trail will take you across both Soda Butte and Amphitheater Creeks. There's no trail along Amphitheater, and you have to maneuver your way around the endless downed timber. Casting is difficult. Fishing is spotty for 8-inch cutthroats, but once in a while you'll be surprised by a 12-incher.

Antelope Creek (Map 5)

BROOK TROUT

This small tributary to the Yellowstone River, reached by taking the trail down to the river at the base of Tower Falls, offers poor fishing for 6-inch brook trout. Nearby Tower Falls and the Grand Canyon of the Yellowstone are much more impressive than the fishing in this little creek.

Bear Creek (Map 7)

CUTTHROAT

As you might surmise from its name, this small creek, which enters Turbid Lake from the south, is deep in the heart of grizzly bear country. It's best reached by following the Turbid Lake Trail east to the lake, then hiking around the lake to the southeast, where you'll find Bear Creek and the primitive Bear Creek Trail. Fishing is okay for cutthroat averaging 6 inches. Turbid Lake—poisonous due to highly acidic geothermal action—prevents any large cutthroat from moving up from Yellowstone Lake.

Bluff Creek (Map 7)

CUTTHROAT

A tributary to Sour Creek, Bluff Creek lies on the east side of the Yellowstone River, across from Hayden Valley. Yellowstone cutthroats spawn here, and it's closed to angling.

Bog Creek (Map 7)

CUTTHROAT

This Sour Creek tributary is a spawning stream for Yellowstone cutthroats and is closed to angling.

Broad Creek (Map 6)

CUTTHROAT

This fair-sized tributary of the Yellowstone River holds cutthroat trout that average 12 inches and is seldom fished. It drains a large part of Mirror Plateau, east of Yellowstone River's Grand Canyon. The lower creek, and its tributaries Shallow and Wrong Creeks, all flow through steep, narrow, remote canyons, and thus are seldom visited. Access is via a 14-mile hike on the Wapiti Lake Trail, which starts at Artist Point, an overlook to the lower falls of the Yellowstone River south of Canyon Junction. You'll want to fish the upper reaches of Broad Creek downstream to Joseph Coat Springs, a distance of 5 miles. Below the springs the stream enters a narrow, steep canyon, and both fishing and access become more difficult. The same is true of its tributaries, Shallow and Wrong Creeks, which enter Broad Creek from the east. This area is home to many of the Park's grizzly bears.

Buffalo Creek (Map 6)

BROOK TROUT • CUTTHROAT

Offering fair fishing for cutthroat and brook trout in the 8-inch range, Buffalo Creek enters Slough Creek directly across from the Slough Creek campground. This small tributary gets quite a bit of pressure near the campground, but the fishing improves the farther you hike upstream. The creek flows steeply down from Buffalo Plateau through a narrow, rocky canyon—an adventurous hike for small fish.

Burnt Creek (Map 5)

CUTTHROAT

To reach this small tributary to Deep Creek, take the Specimen Ridge–Agate Creek Trail for 6 miles to Agate Creek. The trail begins ½ mile east of the Cooke City Bridge, on the Northeast Entrance Highway. Once you reach Agate Creek, you must strike out on your own along the Yellowstone River to reach the mouth of Deep Creek. Follow this upstream another 1½ miles to reach Burnt Creek, which lies in a steep, narrow canyon and has a sparse population of small cutthroat trout. Think twice before taking this hike.

Cache Creek (Map 6)

CUTTHROAT • RAINBOW TROUT

A major tributary to the Lamar River, Cache Creek is accessible by hiking the Lamar River Trail, found near Soda Butte, 14 miles south of the Northeast Entrance on the Northeast Entrance Highway. Follow the Lamar River Trail south for about 3 miles and you'll reach the lower end of Cache Creek itself. If you wish to hike upstream via the trail rather than up the creek, take the Cache Creek Trail (it's marked), about ¼ mile before you reach the creek.

Cache Creek contains a fine population of both cutthroat and rainbow trout of up to 13 inches. This is one of the few small streams in Yellowstone Park with reliable hatches. Green Drakes, Pale Morning Duns, and *Heptagenia* mayflies, along with several caddis species, provide the hiking angler with good dry-fly fishing during July and August. Come September, look for good ant, beetle, and grasshopper fishing.

Calfee Creek (Map 6)

CUTTHROAT

This small tributary enters the Lamar River 4 miles upstream from Cache Creek, and you can find it by following the directions to Cache Creek. Calfee Creek has a good fishery for 8- to 9-inch cutthroats, but the 8½-mile hike puts it beyond a day trip. Plan to overnight, and be wary of both moose and grizzly bears—as you should on any of the streams in the Lamar River drainage, from here on upstream.

Chalcedony Creek (Map 6)

CUTTHROAT

There are a few small cutthroats near the mouth of this tiny creek, which enters the Lamar River 2 miles upstream of the confluence of the Lamar and Soda Butte Creek, but it's really pointless to bother fishing it.

Clover Creek (Map 6)

CUTTHROAT

This tiny stream enters the upper Lamar River from the west, 1½ miles upstream from Miller Creek. Tiny cutthroats can be found near its mouth, but we don't consider it fishable.

Cold Creek (Map 6)

CUTTHROAT

This tributary, near the headwaters of the Lamar River, offers good fishing for 9- to 10-inch cutthroats, but it's a 17½-mile hike into some extremely remote country. Take the Lamar River Trail, found near Soda Butte, 14 miles south of the Northeast Entrance, on the Northeast Entrance Highway. You can also get here by hiking overland from Yellowstone Lake via the Mist Creek Trail. Either way, view this more as a beautiful multiday hike than as a fishing opportunity.

Cottongrass Creek (Map 7)

CUTTHROAT

This small tributary to the Yellowstone enters the river from the east, across Hayden Valley just upstream of Sour Creek. It can be reached by the Howard Eaton Trail; but because it's a spawning stream for Yellowstone cutthroats, it's closed to fishing.

Cottonwood Creek (Map 5)

CUTTHROAT

This fine cutthroat stream is located in the Black Canyon of the Yellowstone River, halfway between the Hellroaring Creek Trail and the Blacktail Deer Creek Trail. The Hellroaring Creek Trailhead is 4 miles west of Tower Junction, on the Mammoth-Tower Highway. Follow this trail north until it connects with the Yellowstone River Trail, then take a left and head west for about 3 miles, cross over Little Cottonwood Creek, and walk another mile to Cottonwood Creek. You can also reach the creek by taking the Blacktail Deer Creek Trail, located 7 miles east of Mammoth on the Mammoth-Tower Highway. It's 4 miles down the trail to the Yellowstone River, then another 3 miles east on the Yellowstone River Trail to Cottonwood Creek.

This creek has good fishing for cutthroat trout averaging 12 inches, with larger cutts possible. It receives little angling pressure due to the long hike and the grizzly bears. We've been treed by a grizzly near this stream.

Coyote Creek (Map 5)

CUTTHROAT • RAINBOW TROUT

This small mountain stream flows into Hellroaring Creek about 2 miles from the Park's north boundary. From the Hellroaring Creek Trailhead, 4 miles west of Tower Junction on the Mammoth-Tower Highway, go north for 2 miles until you connect with the Coyote Creek Trail. From there it's north about 4 more miles to Coyote Creek. This is strictly a small stream–small trout proposition, with mostly cutthroats and a possible rainbow. The fish average 9 inches.

Crevice Creek (Map 5)

CUTTHROAT

From the Mammoth-Tower Highway, take the Blacktail Deer Creek Trail 4 miles north, until it crosses the Yellowstone River at the Blacktail Deer Bridge. After crossing, bear left and follow the trail about a mile west to arrive at Crevice Creek. This tiny, boulder-strewn creek flows down the hillside; it has a sparse population of 8-inch cutthroats below the footbridge, and nothing much above the bridge. Near the mouth of the creek, large cutthroat trout are sometimes found, seeking relief from the heavy flow of the river.

Crystal Creek (Map 6)

CUTTHROAT

This tiny creek, which enters the Lamar River near the Lamar River Bridge, has a few tiny cutthroats, but it isn't a viable fishery in our opinion.

Deep Creek (Map 5)

CUTTHROAT

This Yellowstone River tributary lies deep in a canyon about 5 miles south of the Northeast Entrance Highway, near the Agate Creek Trail. The trailhead lies ½ mile east of the Cooke City Bridge. You'll find most fish near the creek's confluence with the Yellowstone. The resident cutthroat trout are small, but at times you'll find some larger run-up fish from the river. As with its tributary, Burnt Creek, we feel this stream is best left to the grizzly bears.

Elk Creek (Map 5)

BROOK TROUT

Elk Creek crosses the Mammoth-Tower Road 3 miles west of Tower Junction, and it provides good fishing for 8-inch brook trout. The Garnet Hill Trail follows the creek to its confluence with the Yellowstone River. Its tributary, Lost Creek, enters about 2 miles upstream.

Elk Antler Creek (Map 7)

CUTTHROAT

Crossed by the Canyon–Fishing Bridge Highway in Hayden Valley, Elk Antler Creek is used as a spawning stream for Yellowstone cutthroats and is closed to angling.

Elk Tongue Creek (Map 6)

CUTTHROAT

A tributary to Slough Creek, Elk Tongue Creek is the dividing line between the second and third meadows of Slough Creek. Follow the Slough Creek Trail for 7 miles and you'll come to a backcountry patrol cabin and Elk Tongue Creek. The creek itself offers poor-to-nonexistent fishing for small cutthroats, but large Slough Creek cutts can be found near its mouth. Slough Creek is the destination here, not Elk Tongue Creek.

Flint Creek (Map 6)

CUTTHROAT

This tiny tributary to the upper Lamar River enters from the west, just downstream of Calfee Creek. We don't consider this a viable fishery, even though there are tiny cutthroats near its mouth.

Hellroaring Creek (Map 5)

CUTTHROAT • RAINBOW TROUT

This medium-sized tributary to the Yellowstone River is accessible via the Hellroaring Creek Trail, found 3½ miles west of Tower Junction on the Mammoth-Tower Highway. After hiking downhill 1½ miles, you'll cross the suspension bridge over the Yellowstone River. Continue for another ½ mile and you'll connect with the Yellowstone River Trail, which takes you west the final ½ mile to Hellroaring Creek. The fishing is mainly for 10-inch cutthroat and rainbow trout, although larger cutts migrating up from the Yellowstone can be found in the lower creek. Fishing the Yellowstone River at its confluence with Hellroaring Creek, we've taken cutthroat, brook, brown, and rainbow trout along with the occasional mountain whitefish. This is a pleasant day trip that offers a nice blend of scenery, feisty trout, and solitude.

Jasper Creek

Fishless.

Lamar River (Map 6)

CUTTHROAT • RAINBOW TROUT

The Lamar River begins its long journey out of Hoodoo Basin high up in the rugged Absarokas, on the east edge of Yellowstone Park. The river carves its way through 30 miles of canyon, dropping nearly 100 feet per mile. A number of small tributaries enter the Lamar from both sides of the canyon, transforming this small, tumbling, mountain stream into a blue-ribbon meadow river by the time it joins Soda Butte Creek, at the head of Lamar Valley.

This long upper stretch of the Lamar is home to small cutthroats, as the sharp drop in elevation makes the habitat unsuitable for larger trout. The better habitat lies downstream of the canyon. The river is always the last one in the Park to clear from snowmelt, and it usually isn't fishable until late July or early August. Even then, frequent summer thunderstorms in the Absarokas will turn the river muddy for two or three days. If you're fortunate enough to be here the day it clears, the fish will make you beg for mercy.

The canyon ends and the meadow section begins at the Junction Pool, where the Lamar River joins with Soda

Lamar River

Butte Creek. For the next 6 miles, the river flows through one of the most beautiful valley meadows you'll ever see; it's paralleled by the Cooke City Highway. Bison and pronghorns are easily found grazing along the river's banks, but the cutthroat, rainbow, and cuttbow hybrid inhabitants are not so easily found. They have a reputation for migrating—here today, gone tomorrow. A run that was productive one week will seem fishless the next. While this may be abnormal on most streams, it's normal on the Lamar, and when it happens you must start covering water to find the fish. Once you find the trout, you may not have to move again for a while.

The average trout in the meadow section is 15 inches long and readily takes dry flies and nymphs. The Lamar is known primarily as an attractor-fly and terrestrial stream, but you may encounter a few hatches. Of these, the only one you can count on is the Green Drake hatch of late summer. These are often confused with Brown or Gray Drakes, because this Green Drake isn't really green. It's a member of the Green Drake family, but it varies in color from tan to gray. The trout don't seem to care; they gobble up virtually every one that floats downstream. Hatches of this Green Drake are fragmented and seldom heavy, but they're consistent. All it takes is a little effort to patrol the river for this emergence.

The big draw on the Lamar is always its late-summer terrestrial fishing. We say "big" because the insects are *big*. The grassy meadows along the banks of the river produce some enormous grasshoppers, beetles, and—especially— Mormon Crickets. We're sometimes embarrassed when people look into our fly boxes and shudder at the size of the flies we use. Crickets and grasshoppers 2 to 3 inches long and beetles the size of a nickel are crammed into fly boxes set aside only for this river.

At the end of the meadow, the river enters the lower Lamar Canyon, a 6-mile piece of water that finally merges with the Yellowstone River at Black Canyon. The lower canyon is split into two sections by the Lamar River Bridge on the Cooke City Highway. Above the bridge the river is easily accessible from the main road. This narrow canyon produces some nice cutthroats, rainbows, and hybrids if you get deep with big Golden Stonefly nymphs or sculpin patterns. This method will produce the best fish, but the dry-fly fisher can also do well with large attractors and terrestrials worked among the big boulders.

Below the Lamar River Bridge the river curves away from the road on its way to the Yellowstone River; it can only be reached by hiking. While this section of the canyon is scenic, the fishing isn't particularly noteworthy. Poor habitat and small fish are scattered throughout this otherwise lovely canyon. We view this as hiking and not really fishing.

The meadow section of the Lamar was called Paradise Valley by fur trapper Osborne Russell in his 1830s diary, *Journal of a Trapper* (University of Nebraska Press, Lincoln, NE, 1965). Fly fishers would agree with this even today, which is why the Lamar River is one of the most popular streams in Yellowstone Park.

SELECTED EMERGENCES

MAYFLIES

SPECIES	MAY	JUNE	JULY	AUG.	SEPT.	OCT.
BAETIS	|	|	|	|	███████	|
CALLIBAETIS	|	|	|	████████	|	|
EPEORUS	|	|	|	████████	|	|
GREEN DRAKE	|	|	|	|	███████	|
HEPTAGENIA	|	|	|	|	███████	|

CADDIS

SPECIES	MAY	JUNE	JULY	AUG.	SEPT.	OCT.
BRACHYCENTRUS	|	|	|	██████████		|
HYDROPSYCHE	|	|	|	██████████		|
RHYACOPHILA	|	|	|	██████████		|

STONEFLIES

SPECIES	MAY	JUNE	JULY	AUG.	SEPT.	OCT.
SALMONFLY	|	|	|	████	|	|	|
GOLDEN STONEFLY	|	|	|	████	|	|	|

TERRESTRIALS

SPECIES	MAY	JUNE	JULY	AUG.	SEPT.	OCT.
ANTS, BEETLES, MORMON CRICKETS, AND GRASSHOPPERS	|	|	████████████			|

SELECTED FLY PATTERNS

MAYFLIES

BAETIS

PHEASANT TAIL NYMPH, #18–#20

BAETIS NYMPH, #18–#20

BAETIS SPARKLE DUN AND BIPLANE (CRIPPLE), #20–#22

CALLIBAETIS

CALLIBAETIS SPARKLE DUN, #16

ADAMS PARACHUTE, #16

EPEORUS

PARTRIDGE & PRIMROSE SOFT HACKLE, #16

PINK LADY SPARKLE DUN OR SPARKLE DUN, OLIVE, #16–#18

GREEN DRAKE

DRAKE MACKEREL EMERGER, #12

DRAKE MACKEREL SPARKLE DUN, #10–#12

HEPTAGENIA

> PARTRIDGE & PRIMROSE SOFT HACKLE, #14
>
> SULFUR OR CAHILL SPARKLE DUN, #16

CADDIS

> PEACOCK & STARLING SOFT HACKLE, #16
>
> PHEASANT TAIL SOFT HACKLE, #14–#16
>
> X-CADDIS OR ELK HAIR CADDIS, OLIVE AND TAN, #14–#16

STONEFLIES

> BROOKS' BLACK STONE NYMPH, #4–#8
>
> NICK'S GOLDEN STONE NYMPH, #6–#8
>
> KAUFMANN'S STIMULATOR, #6–#8

TERRESTRIALS

> FOAM AND YELLOWSTONE FLYING ANTS, #12–#20
>
> PARACHUTE AND MAGNUM HOPPERS, #4–#10
>
> FOAM BEETLE STANDARD, CRYSTAL, #6–#16
>
> SLOUGH CREEK CRICKET, #4–#8

ATTRACTORS

> ADAMS, #14–#20
>
> H&L VARIANT, #10–#16
>
> POLY GOOFUS, #20
>
> ROYAL WULFF, #8–#18

STREAMERS

> WOOLHEAD SCULPIN, BLACK AND OLIVE, #6
>
> MUDDLER MINNOW, #6–#10
>
> CRYSTAL BUGGER, #6

Terrestrials (from left):
Slough Creek Cricket, Parachute Hopper Foam Beetle, Kaufmanns's Stimulator

Little Buffalo Creek (Map 5)

This tributary to the Yellowstone River flows steeply down Buffalo Plateau, just east of Hellroaring Creek. It's reported to contain fish, but we've hiked it top to bottom with no sign of a trout.

Little Cottonwood Creek (Map 5)

CUTTHROAT

This small tributary to the Yellowstone River is reached over the Hellroaring Creek Trail, 4 miles west of Tower Junction. Take the trail north for 2 miles until you reach the Yellowstone River Trail. Follow this west along the Yellowstone River for 3 miles and you'll reach Little Cottonwood Creek. The cutthroats here are small. The fishing is much better in Cottonwood Creek.

Little Lamar River (Map 6)

CUTTHROAT

Part of the headwaters of the Lamar River, this stream has 6- to 8-inch cutthroats for the angler who dares to make such a long hike—23 miles. Follow the Lamar River Trail almost to its end and you'll see the Little Lamar River entering from the south. This stream receives little pressure. Your only companions will be an occasional bear or moose.

Lost Creek (Map 5)

BROOK TROUT

A tributary to Elk Creek, Lost Creek is a fine brook trout fishery that can be reached by the Garnet Hill Trail. The creek crosses the Mammoth-Tower Highway near Tower Junction and the Roosevelt Lodge, then flows west for about 2 miles before it enters Elk Creek. Plump 8-inch brookies come readily to terrestrials and attractor flies, such as Goofus Bugs and Royal Trudes.

Miller Creek (Map 6)

CUTTHROAT

This tributary to the upper Lamar River enters from the east, 5 miles upstream from Cache Creek. Follow the directions to Cache Creek, but continue along the Lamar River Trail until you cross Miller Creek. There's good fishing for 10-inch cutthroats here, and the trout aren't too selective; they'll take whatever dry fly you throw at them. The creek does experience a few hatches, but an Adams or an Elk Hair Caddis, size 12-16, will suffice. Be sure to bring plenty of grasshopper patterns. This 9-mile hike requires an overnight stay.

Mist Creek (Map 6)

CUTTHROAT

This tributary to the upper Lamar River, entering from the south near its headwaters, is seldom fished. Mist Creek is usually reached by hiking up the Lamar River Trail. However, if you plan to fish this creek only, it's best to take the Mist Creek Trail from the Yellowstone Lake area, which parallels the creek along its descent to the Lamar. Start at the Turbid Lake Trailhead, found ⅓ mile east along the spur road that leaves the Fishing Bridge–East Entrance Highway, 3 miles east of Fishing Bridge. It's then a 3-mile hike to the junction with the Mist Creek Trail, which takes you northeast to the Lamar River. The creek offers good fishing for surprisingly large cutthroats, with trout in the 11- to 12-inch range common. This is a fun choice for anglers wanting an extended day trip. Be sure to take precautions for moose and grizzly bears.

Opal Creek (Map 6)

Technically there are some small cutthroats here, but it isn't a viable fishery.

Otter Creek (Map 7)

Located 3 miles south of Canyon Junction, this small tributary enters the Yellowstone River from the west, on the Canyon–Fishing Bridge Highway. This creek is used primarily as a spawning stream for the Yellowstone's cutthroats, but it does have a few resident trout averaging around 8 inches. Every now and then you may see larger fish move in from the Yellowstone. Oddly enough, this creek is open to fishing, unlike the other spawning streams in the immediate area.

Pelican Creek (Map 7)

This major tributary enters Yellowstone Lake on its north shore. The first 2 miles upstream from the lake are closed to fishing to protect spawning habitat, so plan to hike the Pelican Creek Trail to get to fishable water. The trailhead is found 3 miles east of Fishing Bridge, across from Indian Pond, ⅓ mile down the access road that leaves the Fishing Bridge–East Entrance Highway; it's on the north side of the road. Take the Pelican Creek Trail northeast until the Pelican Valley opens up before you, a distance of about 2 miles. From this point you can fish either upstream or down for cutthroats that average 13 inches. This meandering meadow stream lies in treeless Pelican Valley, and it's prime grizzly bear country. Groups of four or more hikers are required for this trip.

Pelican Creek is primarily a spawning stream, but the fishing is good when the creek opens on July 15. By late August the majority of trout have returned to the lake, though, and the fishing becomes quite difficult under the late summer sun. Gray Drakes and PMDs provide fishable hatches on this stream, but we've always found that the fish rise to terrestrial patterns better than to any other flies.

Pebble Creek (Map 6)

CUTTHROAT • RAINBOW TROUT

Originally named "White Pebble Creek" because of the chalky white sedimentary pebbles found at its headwaters, this fine tributary to Soda Butte Creek enters the stream at Round Prairie, 10 miles south of the Northeast Entrance, on the Northeast Entrance Highway. The Pebble Creek campground is next to the creek, and upstream for ½ mile from the campground, fishing is productive of cutthroat and the occasional rainbow trout, which average 9 inches. Beyond this point the creek winds its way upstream through a steep, trailless canyon that's difficult to hike. The Pebble Creek Trail parallels the creek, but it sits atop a high ridge that makes it useless for stream access.

Anglers wanting to fish the upper meadows should take the Pebble Creek Trail from its north trailhead, 1¼ miles south of the Northeast Entrance, on the Northeast Entrance Highway. Follow the trail northwest for about 2 miles and you'll come to the upper meadows of Pebble Creek. Fishing can be good here for cutthroats that run 10 to 14 inches.

Plateau Creek (Map 6)

This small tributary enters Slough Creek from the south in its second meadow. For all practical purposes this stream is fishless.

Pebble Creek

Quartz Creek (Map 6)

CUTTHROAT

Quartz Creek is a small tributary that enters the Yellowstone River from Specimen Ridge. It's reached by taking the Specimen Ridge–Agate Creek Trail, located ½ mile east of the Cooke City Bridge on the Northeast Entrance Highway. The trail crosses the creek about 3 miles from the trailhead, at the top corner of Mirror Plateau. Downstream from the trail, the stream drops steeply down the side of the Grand Canyon of the Yellowstone, and provides marginal fishing for cutthroat trout at its confluence with the Yellowstone. We don't recommend this trailless hike down the Grand Canyon.

Raven Creek (Map 7)

CUTTHROAT

A small tributary to Pelican Creek, Raven Creek is reached by following the Pelican Creek Trail 7 miles to the Pelican Springs patrol cabin. (See *Pelican Creek* for directions to the Pelican Creek Trail.) Then go west to meet the Pelican Cone Trail and you'll cross Raven Creek after an easy 1-mile walk. This productive stream contains cutthroat trout that often reach 16 inches, but it should be approached and fished with extreme caution, as it's in an area of high grizzly bear activity.

Rose Creek (Map 6)

CUTTHROAT

This tiny tributary to the Lamar River flows past the Yellowstone Institute. Formerly a ranger station, it was originally constructed to breed 21 bison that were purchased by Congress to replenish devastated bison herds, which by the early 1900s had sunk to a worldwide low of 1,700 animals. Rose Creek and the Yellowstone Institute are 11 miles northeast of Tower Junction on the Northeast Entrance Highway. Loads of 6-inch cutthroat trout inhabit the little stream; a 7-incher is a trophy here.

Sedge Creek (Map 7)

CUTTHROAT

This unique fishery flows into and out of Turbid Lake. The creek is reached via the Turbid Lake Trail, which is 3 miles east of Fishing Bridge, across from Indian Pond, ⅓ mile down the access road that leaves the Fishing Bridge–East Entrance Highway; it's on the north side of the road. Follow the Turbid Lake Trail 3 miles to the lake; you'll find Sedge Creek entering the lake from the north. There's no trail along the creek.

Turbid Lake spills its waters—toxic due to highly acidic geothermal action—into the lower portion of Sedge Creek, and both the lake and the lower creek are fishless. Turbid Lake has not always been poisonous, however, and upper Sedge Creek hosts a good population of cutthroat trout forever trapped upstream by the waters of the lifeless lake. Through isolation, they're now considered a separate subspecies of the Yellowstone cutthroat—the Sedge Creek cutthroat. Yellowstone cutthroats have black spots along the entire length of their dorsal, but Sedge Creek cutthroats are spotted only on the tail section of their dorsal. These are special fish! They're small, 7 to 8 inches, but their uniqueness as a separate subspecies adds incentive to this hike.

Shallow Creek (Map 6)

CUTTHROAT

This tributary to Broad Creek holds small cutthroat trout. There's no trail here; access is by hiking off-trail from Wapiti Lake. Small fish and big bears ensure solitude.

Slough Creek (Map 6)

CUTTHROAT • RAINBOW TROUT

Slough Creek is a tributary to the Lamar River located just north of the Lamar River Bridge on the Cooke City Highway, in the northeast corner of Yellowstone Park. Slough (pronounced "sloo") Creek rises in the Beartooth

Mountains of Montana and enters the Park at its north boundary, 11 miles upstream of the Slough Creek campground. The only access to the creek is via the campground road. If you wish to fish either up- or downstream of the campground, you'll have to hike.

To reach the upstream waters, don't hike the stream up from the campground; it travels through a nasty gorge better suited to rock climbers. Instead, start from the trailhead found about ¼ mile before the campground. Look for the outhouse and trail marker; this is the parking area and trailhead for the upper meadows. There are usually cars parked here, because this is also the access to the private Silver Tip Ranch, located just outside the Park's north boundary. The ranch is permitted to use horse-drawn wagons to carry passengers and supplies because it was in existence before the Park was, and this is the wagons' only access. These wagons are used for ranch purposes only; they do *not* provide trail rides, so please respect their privacy and don't ask.

The area above the campground is divided into three meadows. Plan on a comfortable one-hour hike to the first meadow, two hours to the second, and three hours to the third meadow. The meadows are separated by obvious landmarks. The first meadow features patrol cabins on its south hill; the stream is on your left when going upstream. You can't miss the second meadow; the trees on your left give way to a meadow that opens before your eyes as you walk down the hill. The third meadow begins at the patrol cabin on Elk Tongue Creek, which crosses the trail.

The three meadows contain cutthroat and a sparse population of rainbow trout. All the meadows hold roughly the same numbers and sizes of fish, the difference being that the farther you hike, the fewer people you'll see. You won't need to pack in waders here; the only reason to enter the water is to cross the stream. The fish are less sophisticated in the second and third meadows, so matching the hatch isn't critical, but you'd better be prepared to match hatches in the first meadow. The fish will rise to your fly provided you concentrate, exercise patience, and use a fly pattern that matches the natural that they're taking. They aren't necessarily difficult in the first meadow, but they do want things their way. The fun here is catering to their whims.

At the bottom of the first meadow, the river quickly tapers into a gorge, changing from a calm meadow stream to a raging cascade. Take our advice and stay on the trail, for it's the shortest way to the campground.

Slough Creek

For a few hundred yards below the Slough Creek campground there's a nice piece of rough-and-tumble water, ideal stonefly habitat. During July, stonefly nymphs and dries fished through the heavy water often yield surprising results. After these riffles, the stream regains its meadow character for the last 3 miles before it enters the Lamar River. Although this water looks similar to that in the upper meadows, there are some big differences. The stream is much larger and deeper here than it is above. Insect life is much more abundant, varied, and consistent, and the trout take advantage of this increased food supply. Even the fish are different. While cutthroats have the edge in numbers, rainbows and cuttbow hybrids dominate in size. These fish can be as hard to fool as any spring-creek trout.

The nature of this lower water breeds selective trout. It's slow and clear, with multiple currents that lead to immediate drag. These fish have every opportunity to inspect their prey prior to feeding, and they pass up as many naturals as they do imitations. The trout tend to cruise, patrolling the cross-currents, whirlpools, and slack water along the edges, searching for food. Insects collect in the deadwater of back eddies, mixing with foam and other debris. Fish move into the eddies, gulping insects from the foam and scum lines. It's not unusual to locate feeding trout strictly by the sounds of their gulping. Quite often you'll find these gulpers in 6 inches of water.

Lepidostoma

The entire stream holds excellent populations of *Baetis,* PMDs, and Gray and Green Drakes. Caddis include *Brachycentrus, Lepidostoma,* and *Helicopsyche.* Stoneflies present are the Salmonfly, Golden Stonefly, and Little Yellow Stone. Midges are very important here. Trout thought to be taking the obvious small mayfly duns or spinners may be sipping midge pupae just under the surface. Grasshoppers, beetles, ants, and crickets all have their moment in the sun. Of special note are the flying ant swarms in August, which trigger a feeding frenzy. What appears to be barren water suddenly changes to feeding time at the hatchery. We've actually seen trout bobbing vertically for ants, their heads popping out of the water in unison. Unfortunately, few anglers are ever prepared for this unusual event.

Slough Creek is one of our favorite streams, and we're not alone in that. Nestled at the foot of the Beartooths, where mountains snag the clouds, Slough Creek purls its way through four meadows and some of the most spectacular scenery in Yellowstone Park. As good as the fishing is, it's only half the story.

SELECTED EMERGENCES

MAYFLIES

SPECIES	MAY	JUNE	JULY	AUG.	SEPT.	OCT.
BAETIS			████████████████████████
PALE MORNING DUN			███████			
GRAY DRAKE			████████████████		
GREEN DRAKE				██████████████		

CADDIS

SPECIES	MAY	JUNE	JULY	AUG.	SEPT.	OCT.
BRACHYCENTRUS			████████████████		
LEPIDOSTOMA			████████████████		
HELICOPSYCHE			████████████████		

Lepidostoma is the hatch we most often encounter and fish.

STONEFLIES

SPECIES	MAY	JUNE	JULY	AUG.	SEPT.	OCT.
SALMONFLY			██████			
GOLDEN STONEFLY			██████			
LITTLE YELLOW STONE			██████████			

MIDGES

SPECIES	MAY	JUNE	JULY	AUG.	SEPT.	OCT.
SEVERAL SPECIES			████████████████████	

TERRESTRIALS

SPECIES	MAY	JUNE	JULY	AUG.	SEPT.	OCT.
ANTS, FLYING ANTS, BEETLES,			██████████████████████████

MORMON CRICKETS, AND GRASSHOPPERS

Golden Stonefly

SELECTED FLY PATTERNS

MAYFLIES

BAETIS

PHEASANT TAIL NYMPH, #20

BAETIS NYMPH, #20–#22

BAETIS SPARKLE DUN, #20–#22

BIPLANE (CRIPPLE), #20–#22

PALE MORNING DUN (PMD)

PMD NYMPH, #18

PMD EMERGER #18

PMD SPARKLE DUN, #18

PMD BIPLANE (CRIPPLE), #18

PMD RUSTY AND OLIVE SPARKLE SPINNER, #18

GRAY DRAKE

GRAY DRAKE PARADRAKE AND HACKLE-FIBER SPINNER, #12–#14

GREEN DRAKE

DRAKE MACKEREL EMERGER, #12

DRAKE MACKEREL SPARKLE DUN, #10–#12

CADDIS

X-CADDIS, OLIVE, #18

STONEFLIES

BROOKS' BLACK STONE NYMPH, #6–#8

KAUFMANN'S AMBER SEAL STONE NYMPH, #8–#10

HENRY'S FORK SALMONFLY, #6

KAUFMANN'S STIMULATOR, #8–#16

MIDGES

SERENDIPITY, BROWN, CRYSTAL, OLIVE, #16–#22

SLOUGH CREEK MIDGE, #16–#20

HORSE HAIR MIDGE PUPA, #16–#20

Z-LON MIDGE (CRIPPLE), #20–#22

POLY GOOFUS, #20

ATTRACTORS

NOT RECOMMENDED

TERRESTRIALS

DAVE'S AND PARACHUTE HOPPERS, #8–#14

YELLOWSTONE FLYING ANT, #12–#14

Z-LON FLYING ANT, #18

FOAM BEETLE, #12–#18

SLOUGH CREEK CRICKET, #6–#8

Soda Butte Creek (Map 6)

CUTTHROAT • RAINBOW TROUT

This large tributary to the Lamar River parallels the Northeast Entrance Highway, from the Northeast Entrance to the stream's confluence with the Lamar, a distance of 15 road miles. Soda Butte Creek is a mountain stream in its upper reaches, containing 10-inch rainbows and cutthroats, but it changes character downstream from Icebox Canyon. The tree line now gives way to meadows, and the fish range from 12 to 14 inches. In this stretch, hatches of Green Drakes, *Baetis,* and PMDs produce fine rises of trout nearly every day during July, August, and September. Terrestrial patterns such as crickets, grasshoppers, and beetles are "must-haves" during late summer and early fall.

Soda Butte Creek

South Cache Creek (Map 6)

CUTTHROAT

This small tributary to Cache Creek is reached by following the Lamar River Trail for 3 miles to Cache Creek, then hiking the Cache Creek Trail northeast for 4 miles to South Cache Creek. This trailless mountain creek flows through a canyon at the base of The Needle, 9,907 feet, and offers good fishing for small cutthroat trout.

Sour Creek (Map 7)

CUTTHROAT

This tributary to the Yellowstone River is on the east side of the river across from Hayden Valley. Access is over the Howard Eaton Trail south from the Upper Falls of the Yellowstone. Sour Creek is a spawning stream for Yellowstone cutthroats and is closed to angling.

Thistle Creek (Map 7)

CUTTHROAT

This small tributary to the Yellowstone enters the river from the east, upstream of the LeHardy Rapids. It can be reached over the Howard Eaton Trail and holds small cutthroats in the 6-inch range. But there's no reason to fish this creek with the Yellowstone River so close at hand.

Timothy Creek (Map 6)

CUTTHROAT

Small cutthroats can be found near Timothy Creek's confluence with the upper Lamar River, but in our opinion it isn't a viable fishery.

Trout Creek (Map 7)

CUTTHROAT

Crossed by the Canyon–Fishing Bridge Highway in the Hayden Valley, Trout Creek is a spawning stream for Yellowstone cutthroats and is closed to angling.

Willow Creek (Map 6)

CUTTHROAT

Another of the small tributaries that enter the upper Lamar River from the south, Willow Creek provides some fishing for 6-inch cutthroats near its mouth, but it's hardly a noteworthy fishery.

Wrong Creek (Map 6)

CUTTHROAT

Wrong Creek is the uppermost tributary to Broad Creek and supports a sparse population of small cutthroat trout. It's a good place to see grizzly bears, but not to fish.

Yellowstone River (Map 7)

BROOK TROUT • BROWN TROUT • CUTTHROAT • MOUNTAIN WHITEFISH • RAINBOW TROUT

The Yellowstone River is the showcase of American trout streams—the world's premier cutthroat trout fishery and the longest undammed river in the United States, it has the most prolific insect hatches of any place we know and is the most popular river in the Park for angling and fish watching.

The Yellowstone River begins its long journey to the Missouri River as two small branches in Wyoming's Shoshone Mountain Range, flowing north from 12,000-foot Yount Peak and crossing the south boundary of Yellowstone Park, where it enters the Park's Thorofare region. For the next 14 miles to Yellowstone Lake, the river meanders through the wildest and most primitive country in the lower 48 states. It's surrounded by marshes, bogs, and sloughs, making travel difficult until late summer. Biting flies and mosquitoes can make life uncomfortable in these parts until things dry out. The grizzly bears remain, however.

A trip to the Thorofare demands respect. At best it's two days in, two days out, and you've yet to wet a line. Plan on a minimum 7-day trip; 10 days is best. Hire an experienced outfitter who'll take care of the camping, food, and bears while you tend to more important things, like fishing.

Yellowstone River

This area is untouched, a place of exceptional beauty no different today than when the first fur trapper passed through in the 1700s. The cutthroats here are highly migratory, as the river is primarily a spawning stream for Yellowstone Lake cutts. The trout average 15 to 16 inches and are no more plentiful here than anywhere else on the river. The reason to make this trip is for the scenery and solitude, not necessarily the fishing.

After leaving the Thorofare region, the river enters Yellowstone Lake's southeast arm and exits at Fishing Bridge on the lake's north shore. By now enriched with the waters of many fine cutthroat streams, the Yellowstone becomes one of the largest and best trout streams in the world.

From ¼ mile upstream (south) to 1 mile downstream (north) of Fishing Bridge, the river is permanently closed to fishing. But this is a great place for fish watching, which is currently more popular than fishing on the river. For the next 6 miles, as you journey downstream to Sulphur Caldron, the river is open to catch-and-release fishing for Yellowstone cutthroats. (The only exception is the ½-mile-long study area at LeHardy Rapids, which is halfway between Fishing Bridge and Sulphur Caldron; this is closed to fishing.) At first glance the river here seems slow moving and easy wading, but looks can be deceiving. This current is powerful, and you can easily be swept off your feet if you get careless.

The Yellowstone cutthroat is the only trout in the river from Yellowstone Lake downstream to the Upper Falls, a 13-mile section paralleled by the Lake-Canyon Road. Access is as easy as the drive; there are plenty of turnouts and three picnic areas. The Buffalo Ford picnic area is one of the most popular spots for catching trout that average 16 to 17 inches—and for watching other people catch them. There's no other place in Yellowstone Park so accessible to anglers, including those with physical disabilities.

The water in the river runs cold all year long, and most insect hatches don't begin until 10 A.M., truly gentlemen's hours. We often drive along the road looking for rising trout before deciding on a place to fish, because studies have shown that the cutthroats not only move around in the river, but also move in and out of Yellowstone Lake. Some fish, tracked via radio collar, moved up to 8 miles in 24 hours!

The Yellowstone River is a virtual insect factory. The list of important insects is nearly as long as the river itself. The three most important are Pale Morning Duns, Green

Drakes, and Gray Drakes. Other major mayfly hatches include *Baetis, Rhithrogena,* Flavs, Pink Ladies, *Attenella margarita, Serratella tibialis,* and *Heptagenia solitaria.* Major caddis emergences include *Hydropsyche, Hesperophylax designatus, Micrasema bactro, Lepidostoma pluviale, Brachycentrus americanus,* and *Rhyacophila bifila.* There are Salmonflies and Golden Stoneflies, there are several species of midges that emerge all season long, and the river is loaded with scuds. The banks virtually crawl with grasshoppers, ants, crickets, and—especially—beetles.

Green Drake Nymph

Don't be intimidated by this long list; it's one of the reasons the Yellowstone is the Park's most popular river. One or more insects are usually emerging daily, with staggering numbers of trout rising to them; and while these trout have the reputation of being easy the first two weeks of the season, they soon become very selective. Avoid flock shooting. Pick out a single fish, determine what insect it's eating, and match that with an imitation. To avoid drag, fish the shortest possible line.

Attenella margarita dun

Downstream from Buffalo Ford, just below Sulphur Caldron, the river is reserved as a wildlife-study area and is closed to fishing for the 6 miles down to Alum Creek. From Alum Creek downstream to the Chittenden Bridge, the river grows less productive as it picks up speed, heading to the Upper Falls. Be careful wading here; you're close to the falls and the current is deceptively strong.

Below the falls and all the way to the town of Gardiner, Montana, a distance of about 45 miles, the river cuts through two canyons. Directly below the falls is the Grand Canyon of the Yellowstone, and access to this stretch is very difficult.

Yellowstone River

The least-difficult spot is Seven Mile Hole, a mere 1,500-
foot drop down the canyon wall. The hike down isn't too
bad, but climbing the wall at the end of the day might
make you reconsider. There are cutthroat, brown, brook,
and rainbow trout here, along with some huge whitefish,
but the fish are neither larger nor more plentiful than in the
section below the lake, and the only hatch you're liable to
hit may be the Salmonflies in July.

The Grand Canyon ends and the Black Canyon of the Yellowstone begins at the Cooke City Bridge. For the next 20 miles en route to Gardiner, Montana, the river is remote, brawling canyon water, never closer than a mile to the road. Access to the canyon isn't difficult, but maneuvering around the canyon walls is. There are few trails once you're in the canyon. This is prime grizzly country; take precautions to prevent an encounter. If you like solitude, you'll like it here, but we don't recommend this for a fishing trip.

The Yellowstone River strides across the entire length of Yellowstone Park, with unmatched scenery, solitude, and fishing. The best fishing and the best hatches are found from Yellowstone Lake to Sulphur Caldron. The fun begins on July 15. We'll see you there!

SELECTED EMERGENCES

MAYFLIES

SPECIES	MAY	JUNE	JULY	AUG.	SEPT.	OCT.
BAETIS				■	■	■
RHITHROGENA			■	■		
PALE MORNING DUN			■	■		
GRAY DRAKE			■	■		
GREEN DRAKE			■	■		
FLAV			■	■		
PINK LADY			■	■		
ATTENELLA margarita				■	■	
SERRATELLA tibialis				■	■	
HEPTAGENIA				■		

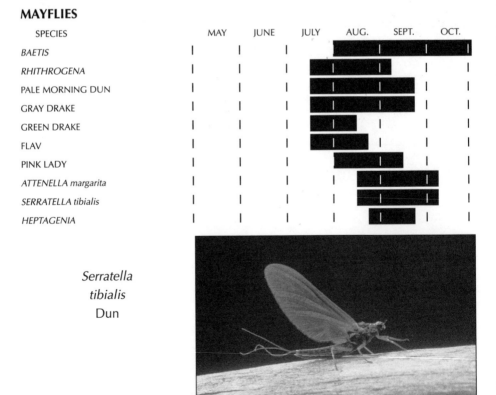

Serratella
tibialis
Dun

Mayflies (from left):
Rusty Spinner,
Gray Drake Spinner,
Biplane,
Sparkle Dun

CADDIS

SPECIES	MAY	JUNE	JULY	AUG.	SEPT.	OCT.
HYDROPSYCHE						
HESPEROPHYLAX designatus						
MICRASEMA bactro						
LEPIDOSTOMA pluviale						
BRACHYCENTRUS americanus						
RHYACOPHILA bifila						

STONEFLIES

SPECIES	MAY	JUNE	JULY	AUG.	SEPT.	OCT.
SALMONFLY						
GOLDEN STONEFLY						

MIDGES

SPECIES	MAY	JUNE	JULY	AUG.	SEPT.	OCT.
SEVERAL SPECIES						

Midges will be found almost anytime during the season.

SCUDS

SPECIES	MAY	JUNE	JULY	AUG.	SEPT.	OCT.
SEVERAL SPECIES						

Scuds will be found almost anytime during the season.

TERRESTRIALS

SPECIES	MAY	JUNE	JULY	AUG.	SEPT.	OCT.
ANTS, BEETLES, CRICKETS, AND GRASSHOPPERS						

SELECTED FLY PATTERNS

MAYFLIES

BAETIS

    BAETIS NYMPH, #18–#22

    PHEASANT TAIL NYMPH, #18–#22

    BAETIS EMERGER, #20–#22

    BAETIS SPARKLE DUN, #20–#22

    BAETIS BIPLANE (CRIPPLE), #20–#22

RHITHROGENA

    OLIVE SPARKLE SPINNER, #16 (ONLY THE SPINNER IMITATION IS REQUIRED)

PALE MORNING DUN (PMD)

    PMD NYMPH, #16–#20

    PHEASANT TAIL NYMPH, #16–#20

    PMD EMERGER, #16–#18

    PMD SPARKLE DUN, #16–#20

    PMD BIPLANE (CRIPPLE), #16–#20

    PMD RUSTY AND OLIVE SPARKLE SPINNER, #16–#20

GREEN DRAKE

    GREEN DRAKE EMERGER, PARADRAKE, SPARKLE DUN, AND SPINNER, #8–#12

FLAV

    FLAV EMERGER, SPARKLE DUN, BIPLANE, AND SPARKLE SPINNER, #14–#16

GRAY DRAKE

    GRAY DRAKE SPARKLE DUN AND HACKLE-FIBER SPINNER, #10–#12

PINK LADY

    PRIMROSE & PARTRIDGE SOFT HACKLE AND SPARKLE DUN, #16

ATTENELLA margarita

    PHEASANT TAIL NYMPH, OLIVE SPARKLE DUN, AND SPARKLE SPINNER, #18

SERRATELLA tibialis

    PHEASANT TAIL NYMPH, SPARKLE DUN, AND SPINNER, #16–#18

HEPTAGENIA solitaria

    SPARKLE DUN, TAN, #16

CADDIS

HYDROPSYCHE

    LAFONTAINE SPARKLE PUPA, IRISE, X-CADDIS, AND ELK HAIR CADDIS, TAN, #14–#16

HESPEROPHYLAX designatus

    KAUFMANN'S STIMULATOR OR ELK HAIR CADDIS, #8–#12

MICRASEMA bactro

    ANTRON PUPA, IRISE, X-CADDIS, AND SPENT

    SPARKLE CADDIS, GREEN, #18–#20

LEPIDOSTOMA

    ANTRON PUPA, X-CADDIS, ELK HAIR CADDIS, AND

    SPENT SPARKLE CADDIS, OLIVE, #18

BRACHYCENTRUS

    PEACOCK & STARLING, #16

    X-CADDIS, OLIVE, #16

    HEMINGWAY CADDIS, #14–#16

RHYACOPHILA

    NICK'S SOFT HACKLE AND X-CADDIS, OLIVE, #14–#16

Caddisflies(from left):
X-Caddis,
Anrtron Caddis Pupa,
Spent Caddis,
Irise Caddis

STONEFLIES

SALMONFLY

    BROOKS' BLACK STONE NYMPH, #4–#8

    KAUFMANN'S SEAL STONE NYMPH, #4–#8

    ORANGE STIMULATOR, #8

    HENRY'S FORK SALMONFLY, #4–#8

GOLDEN STONEFLY

    KAUFMANN'S AMBER SEAL STONE, #6–#10

    GEORGE'S BROWN STONE NYMPH, #6–#10

    HENRY'S FORK GOLDEN STONE AND STIMULATOR, #6–#10

MIDGES

    SERENDIPITY, LIME, OLIVE, GRAY, #18–#22

    Z-LON MIDGE (CRIPPLE), #20–#22

    GRIFFITH'S GNAT, #18–#22

ATTRACTORS

    PRINCE NYMPH, #6–#16

    YELLOWSTONE SCUD, #14–#16

    ADAMS, TRUDE, AND ROYAL AND GRAY WULFFS, #10–#18

TERRESTRIALS

    DAVE'S, PARACHUTE, AND HENRY'S FORK HOPPERS, #10–#14

    FOAM BEETLE, STANDARD, CRYSTAL, #12–#16

    Z-LON AND YELLOWSTONE FLYING ANTS, #16–#18

Yellowstone River

LAKES AND PONDS

Beach Springs Lake

Fishless.

Buck Lake

Fishless.

Clear Lake

Fishless.

Crevice Lake

Fishless.

Dewdrop Lake

Fishless.

Fern Lake (Map 7)

CUTTHROAT

Tiny cutthroat trout are so scarce here that we don't consider Fern Lake a viable fishery.

Foster Lake

Fishless.

Frost Lake

Fishless.

McBride Lake (Map 6)

CUTTHROAT • RAINBOW TROUT

This 23-acre lake has fine populations of cutthroat and rainbow trout that average 12 inches. It's located on the edge of Buffalo Plateau, northeast of Slough Creek's first meadow.

Take the Slough Creek Trail about 2 miles to the first meadow, ford the creek, and proceed northeast across the meadow and toward the lake. There'll be a rocky hill in front of you. Stay to the left around the base of the hill, then angle right, uphill, for ⅓ mile; this will take you to the southwest end of the lake. There's no trail to the lake once you leave the Slough Creek Trail, so carry a topographical map. Backcountry travel is often closed in this area due to grizzly bear activity. Bears are a secondary threat compared to the vicious mosquitoes.

Mirror Lake

Fishless.

Rainy Lake

Fishless.

Ribbon Lake (Map 6)

RAINBOW TROUT

Located just east of the Grand Canyon of the Yellowstone River, Ribbon Lake is reached by a 2-mile hike that begins at Artist Point, 2 miles south of Canyon Junction. The Ribbon Lake Trail takes you along the rim of the Grand Canyon, then through a forest filled with wildflowers. The lake is actually two lakes connected by a short, shallow stream. The smaller lake is very shallow and filled with lily pads, with a marshy shore. The larger lake is also surrounded by a marshy shore, but it's much deeper and offers fair angling for rainbow trout that struggle to reach 7 inches. This is a beautiful hike, but the boggy shoreline makes fishing difficult and suppresses your appetite for casting to the small trout.

Shrimp Lake

Cutthroat trout were stocked here in the 1930s, and at one time the lake produced large fish, but it was unable to sustain the fishery and is now barren.

Tern Lakes

Fishless.

Trout Lake (Map 6)

CUTTHROAT • RAINBOW TROUT

Originally named "Fish Lake," this excellent fishery is found on the west side of the Northeast Entrance Highway, 11 miles south of the Northeast Entrance, and opens to fishing June 15. The 12-acre lake sits just over the hill from the unmarked Trout Lake Trailhead, a ½-mile uphill hike away. This is the first of three lakes in the area; fishless Buck and Shrimp Lakes are nearby. Trout Lake is heavily fished for its cutthroats, rainbows, and cuttbow hybrids, which have been known to approach 10 pounds and 30 inches. Of

Trout Lake

course these are the exceptions. The average trout here runs 16 to 17 inches.

Mostly this lake calls for blind fishing with a nymph, but sometimes you must fish to visible trout cruising just under the surface, taking *Callibaetis* mayfly adults and nymphs.

Trumpeter Lakes

Fishless.

Turbid Lake

Fishless.

Wapiti Lake

Fishless.

White Lakes (Map 7)

CUTTHROAT

These two large lakes at the headwaters of Broad Creek are best reached by following the Pelican Creek Trail to its junction with the Tern Lake Trail. Go north on the Tern Lake Trail for a little over 4 miles and you'll come to the White Lakes on your left. For all practical purposes these shallow lakes should be considered as fishless as neighboring Fern Lake and Tern Lakes, even though there are a few very small cutthroats. This area has high grizzly bear activity.

Wrangler Lake

Fishless.

3

SOUTHEAST

YELLOWSTONE LAKE AND
THE THOROFARE REGION

The southeast corner of Yellowstone National Park is one of the most remote areas in the continental United States. The only roads are along its north and west boundaries. It's over 40 miles as the crow flies from Fishing Bridge on Yellowstone Lake to the Thorofare patrol cabin in the southeast corner of the Park, and there isn't a road anywhere. Throughout this region, travel is mostly by foot trail and boat.

The Yellowstone Lake–Thorofare region contains Eagle Peak, the highest point in the Park, at 11,358 feet; Two Ocean Plateau, where streams drain to both the Atlantic and Pacific Oceans; and Yellowstone Lake, the largest natural freshwater lake in the United States above a 7,000-foot altitude. It's also the headwaters for the Yellowstone River, the longest undammed river in the U.S.

The region contains the largest concentration of grizzly bears in the lower 48 states, as well as elk, moose, wolves, and wolverines. But for fly fishers the big draw is the Yellowstone cutthroat, the only trout native to Yellowstone National Park. This is the world's largest natural cutthroat fishery, and many mammals and birds, like the grizzly bear and bald eagle, rely on the life cycle of this crown jewel of American trout.

RIVERS AND STREAMS

Aster Creek (Map 9)

BROOK TROUT • BROWN TROUT

This small tributary to the Lewis River is just below Lewis River Falls, east of the West Thumb–South Entrance Highway. Aster Creek holds healthy populations of small

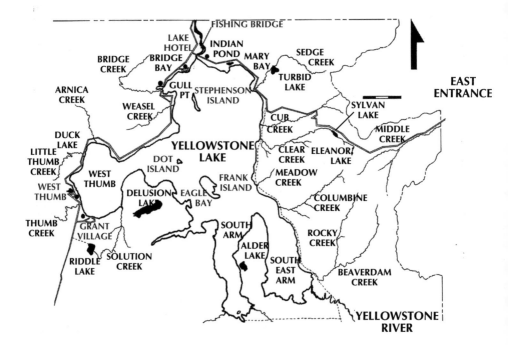

Map 8 — Yellowstone Lake

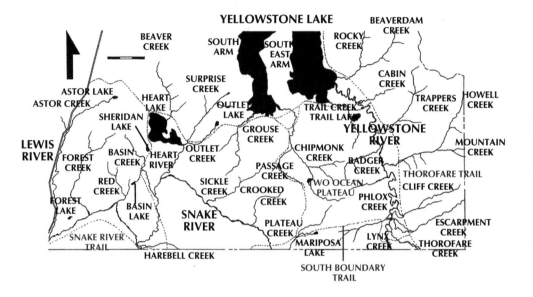

Map 9 — The Thorofare

brook and brown trout that average under 7 inches, and the fishing is fast and furious with small grasshopper patterns during the summer.

Badger Creek (Map 9)

CUTTHROAT

There's no trail access along the marshy shores of this small tributary to the Yellowstone River. Badger Creek enters the river from the west, down a steep grade from Two Ocean Plateau. Yellowstone Lake cutthroats migrate up this creek to spawn, and grizzly bears and bald eagles prey on the spawning trout. It's best to avoid this stream.

Basin Creek (Map 9)

CUTTHROAT

A small cutthroat tributary to the upper Snake River, Basin Creek is seldom fished. The Heart Lake Trail crosses the creek 12 miles southeast of the Heart Lake Trailhead, 7½ miles south of West Thumb, on the West Thumb–South Entrance Highway. You can also reach this creek by following the South Boundary Trail 6 miles to its junction with the Heart Lake Trail; take a left on the Heart Lake Trail and you'll reach the creek in another 5 miles. It's the same distance whichever way you go. The only reason to fish Basin Creek is if you're passing by.

Beaver Creek (Map 9)

CUTTHROAT

The cutthroat trout in this good-sized tributary to Heart Lake run big, averaging around 16 inches. Access it by following the Heart Lake Trail for 7½ miles to Heart Lake, then skirting the north shore of the lake on the Trail Creek Trail for another 2 miles. The long hike and the marshy conditions mean few anglers fish this creek. The cutthroats here are never selective; almost any fly pattern resembling food will work.

Beaverdam Creek (Map 8)

CUTTHROAT

Another of Yellowstone Lake's many spawning streams, Beaverdam Creek has a small population of resident cutthroats, but due to high grizzly bear concentrations there's no reason to make the trip for such small fish. This small tributary is reached by following the Thorofare Trail 18 miles south from its beginning at Lake Butte, 10 miles east of Fishing Bridge, on the East Entrance Highway.

Big Thumb Creek (Map 8)

CUTTHROAT

Big Thumb Creek enters Yellowstone Lake just above Grant Village, on the West Thumb–South Entrance Highway. This is a spawning and nursery stream for Yellowstone Lake cutthroats, and it and its small resident trout are best left unmolested.

Cabin Creek (Map 9)

CUTTHROAT

Yellowstone Lake cutthroats spawn here, but we don't recommend hiking into *any* stream where the patrol cabin has been destroyed by grizzly bears, as this one has.

Chipmunk Creek (Map 9)

CUTTHROAT

Yellowstone Lake cutthroats spawn in this fine stream. Access is from the Thorofare Trail, 20 miles south to Cabin Creek, then another 7 miles west on the Trail Creek Trail. There's a good trail up Chipmunk Creek for several miles from the lake. At times the lower reaches are full of spawning cutthroats, and the fishing is great for both humans and grizzly bears. Four miles upstream from the south arm of Yellowstone Lake, Chipmunk Creek opens up into a marshy meadow and becomes a meandering meadow creek; in dry years there's fine action with terrestrial patterns for resident cutthroats up to a foot long.

Clear Creek (Map 8)

CUTTHROAT

This major tributary to Yellowstone Lake is located 3 miles south of Lake Butte on the Thorofare Trail. Clear Creek is a beautiful stream that provides thousands of cutthroats with a safe place to spawn until late in the season (August). Check the regulations each year, as opening dates change with the spawning seasons and grizzly bear closures. Wherever you find spawning trout, we recommend leaving them be so that they can propagate without the added stress of angling.

Cliff Creek (Map 9)

CUTTHROAT

This small spawning stream enters the Yellowstone River from The Trident, 2 miles north of the Thorofare patrol cabin, 30 miles south on the Thorofare Trail. Its few small, resident cutthroats provide few angling opportunities after the spawning season.

Columbine Creek (Map 8)

CUTTHROAT

Found about 9 miles south of Lake Butte on the Thorofare Trail, Columbine Creek enters Yellowstone Lake from the east. It also forms the upper boundary of special boating regulations on the south and southeast arms of the lake, should you travel by boat. (Check the current boating regulations.)

Columbine Creek is a prime spawning stream for Yellowstone Lake cutthroats. Like other spawning streams in the area, large fish are present only during the spawn, and when it's over, only small trout remain. In high-water years, avoid this creek until August because of flooding. There are grizzly bears everywhere on this stream when the trout are spawning.

Crooked Creek (Map 9)

CUTTHROAT

There's little reason to head into this small cutthroat stream unless you're hiking into another area of the Thorofare region. Crooked Creek is best reached by following the South Boundary Trail. Hike east from its trailhead at the South Entrance for 23 miles until it meets the end of the Snake River Trail. Then follow the Snake River Trail northwest for 4 miles to the creek.

Cub Creek (Map 8)

CUTTHROAT

A 1½-mile hike south from Lake Butte on the Thorofare Trail—found 10 miles east of Fishing Bridge on the Fishing Bridge–East Entrance Highway—will take you to this heavily fished cutthroat spawning stream. Intense grizzly activity forces an opening date in August. Check regulations before making the short hike to this creek. We recommend giving the spawning trout a rest.

Escarpment Creek (Map 9)

CUTTHROAT

Escarpment Creek flows west into the Yellowstone River from The Trident, 31 miles south on the Thorofare Trail, 1 mile above the Thorofare patrol cabin. This little stream supports a small population of resident cutthroats, but it's mainly a spawning stream for fish from the river.

Forest Creek (Map 9)

CUTTHROAT

This pretty little mountain creek enters the Snake River from the north, 5 miles east of the South Entrance, on the South Boundary Trail. Below its canyon and before it enters the Snake River, the creek offers good fishing for small cutthroats. The Snake River must be forded to reach it.

Grouse Creek (Map 9)

CUTTHROAT

Grouse Creek flows east from the Continental Divide, down Chicken Ridge, to the south arm of Yellowstone Lake. Primarily a cutthroat spawning stream, the creek is reached by taking the Heart Lake Trail to its junction with the Trail Creek Trail, then heading east on the latter to Grouse Creek Crossing, a total distance of 17½ miles. The Heart Lake Trailhead is on the West Thumb–South Entrance Highway, 7½ miles south of West Thumb and on the east side of the road.

Harebell Creek (Map 9)

CUTTHROAT

Named after the wildflower *Campanula rotundifolia*, a mountain bluebell lasting late into autumn, this remote stream rises on the southwest side of Big Game Ridge and is reached via a 10½ mile hike east on the South Boundary Trail. This small tributary to the Snake River contains small cutthroat trout.

Heart River (Map 9)

CUTTHROAT

This 4-mile-long outlet of Heart Lake enters the Snake River on the north edge of Big Game Ridge. The Heart is best reached by following the Heart Lake Trail 7½ miles south to Heart Lake, then 4½ miles east to the Heart River Cutoff Trail, a total distance of 12 miles. The river leaves the lake just south of here for its 4-mile trip down to the Snake River. Fishing is good for cutthroat trout that run 8 to 14 inches. The lower end of this river is quite marshy, so we prefer to fish it near its outlet from the lake with *Callibaetis* mayfly imitations.

Howell Creek (Map 9)

CUTTHROAT

Howell Creek supports a fair population of resident cutthroat trout that average 10 inches. At times, spawning trout ascend from the Yellowstone, providing larger fish. Access is by following the Thorofare Trail south from Lake Butte, off the Fishing Bridge–East Entrance Highway, for 26 miles. At the Mountain Creek Trail go east, on your way to Eagle Creek Pass, and after 3 miles you'll find Howell Creek on your right.

Lewis River, below Lewis Lake (Map 9)

BROOK TROUT • BROWN TROUT • LAKE TROUT

This river leaves Lewis Lake 11½ miles north of the South Entrance, on the West Thumb–South Entrance Highway. (Another 4-mile section of the Lewis River, known as the Lewis River Channel, located between Lewis and Shoshone Lakes, is detailed in section 4, *Southwest,* of this book.) The first ¼ mile of river as it comes out of Lewis Lake is easily reached from the Lewis Lake campground and offers good fishing for browns and lake trout, which move in and out of the river. Be sure to bring your bug repellent, as mosquitoes and biting flies are fierce. Below this point and for about a mile downstream to the falls, access is difficult because there's no trail. Downfall timber and steep cliffs make this a place to avoid; it offers poor fishing for small fish.

From its falls downstream to the canyon, the Lewis follows the West Thumb–South Entrance Highway for a little over 2 miles. This stretch is reminiscent of a spring creek, with slow-moving meadow water and large, wary brown trout. Hatches of Pale Morning Duns, Green Drakes, and Flavs, along with several caddis species, will bring these fish to the surface. In the late season, terrestrials also account for some big fish. This is major-league fly fishing. Long leaders, fine tippets, and stalking skills are necessary for success in this section.

When the Lewis River enters its canyon, access is nearly impossible due to the steep canyon walls and rock faces. The river remains in the canyon for several miles, until it joins the Snake River near the South Entrance. Despite repeated attempts, we've never found good fishing in the canyon. The dangers of climbing in and out mean it's best left alone.

Lewis River Canyon

Little Thumb Creek

Fishless.

Lynx Creek (Map 9)

CUTTHROAT

One of the numerous spawning creeks for cutthroat trout in the Thorofare region of the Yellowstone River, Lynx Creek flows east into the river from Two Ocean Plateau. The creek sits in the very southeast corner of Yellowstone Park, roughly equidistant from both the South Boundary Trailhead, 31 miles, and the Thorofare Trailhead, 34 miles. It doesn't matter which trail you take, this trip is only for the hike. It's also in serious bear country.

Meadow Creek (Map 8)

CUTTHROAT

Tiny Meadow Creek enters Yellowstone Lake 15 miles south of Lake Butte on the Thorofare Trail. It's a spawning stream for Yellowstone Lake cutthroats and supports a sparse population of small, resident trout; it isn't worth the time to hike in and fish it.

Lewis River Falls

Middle Creek (Map 8)

BROOK TROUT • CUTTHROAT • RAINBOW TROUT

This small stream has a good population of wild trout. Although the East Entrance Road parallels the creek for nearly its entire length, you'll want to head for the stream near the Park's East Entrance. When the road climbs steeply uphill just west of the entrance, park and begin fishing. Middle Creek has resident brook, cutthroat, and rainbow trout that average 10 inches. Early in the season, after the snowmelt leaves (July), expect to take cutts that run even larger. This is one of the few streams in the area with a good population of the huge October Caddis; a size-8 Orange Stimulator works well.

Mountain Creek (Map 9)

CUTTHROAT

Crossed by the Thorofare Trail 26 miles south of Lake Butte, this spawning stream for Yellowstone Lake cutthroats also has a fishable population of 8-inch cutthroats. Any high-floating attractor dry fly will work; most of the resident fish have never seen an artificial fly.

Outlet Creek (Map 9)

CUTTHROAT

This creek drains Outlet Lake and flows west into the Heart River, near the south shore of Heart Lake. Trail Creek Trail parallels Outlet Creek. There's much better fishing in Heart Lake and other nearby streams, so we don't bother with this small cutthroat fishery.

Passage Creek (Map 9)

CUTTHROAT

A smaller tributary to the already small Chipmunk Creek, Passage Creek is a spawning stream for Yellowstone Lake cutthroats. After mid-July the spawning trout all but disappear back into the lake, leaving behind a diminutive resident population of trout. Passage Creek enters the lake's southeast arm. It's reached by taking the Heart Lake Trail to the Trail Creek Trail, then heading east on the latter to the Passage Creek Cutoff—a total distance of 20½ miles. Also see *Chipmunk Creek.*

Phlox Creek (Map 9)

CUTTHROAT

This short tributary flows east down Two Ocean Plateau to the Yellowstone River. Used by Yellowstone Lake cutthroats as a spawning stream, its resident population of small cutts is best ignored, as there's no trail to the creek and it's in high-frequency bear country.

Plateau Creek (Map 9)

CUTTHROAT

A small tributary to the upper Snake River, Plateau Creek offers marginal fishing for cutthroat trout that average 8 inches. Grizzly bears frequent the creek, and it's reached by a 25-mile hike along the South Boundary Trail. Consider this a hiking destination, not a fishing trip.

Red Creek (Map 9)

CUTTHROAT

This tiny tributary enters the Snake River 6 miles east on the South Boundary Trail and 1 mile north on the Heart Lake Trail. The little resident cutthroats aren't worth the trouble.

Rocky Creek (Map 8)

CUTTHROAT

This tributary to Beaverdam Creek is a mile northeast of the Thorofare Trail, 18 miles south of Lake Butte on the east side of Yellowstone Lake. Rocky Creek is spawning and nursery water for Yellowstone cutthroats, with a resident small-trout population of its own.

Sickle Creek (Map 9)

CUTTHROAT

Follow the South Boundary Trail 9 miles east until you reach the Snake River Trail. Follow this trail north, then east, until you reach the creek, which enters the Snake River from the north, draining Chicken Ridge. There's no reason to make this a destination stream, but it does offer fun fishing for small cutthroat trout if you happen to be passing on your way elsewhere.

Snake River (Map 9)

BROOK TROUT • BROWN TROUT • CUTTHROAT • LAKE TROUT • RAINBOW TROUT • MOUNTAIN WHITEFISH

This remote river gets little angling pressure because of the long hike and its inconsistent fishing. Although a number of trails reach this river, the easiest route is to follow the South Boundary Trail 9 miles east to the Snake River Trail, then follow the latter, which runs along the river's entire length. The trailhead for the South Boundary Trail is located at the South Entrance to the Park. Brook, brown, rainbow, and lake trout are found here, but cutthroats and mountain whitefish make up the majority of fish caught.

Access to the river is more difficult than it appears on a map; much of the stream is in a canyon, with no bridges or trails to get you there. You're on your own. The Snake River Trail from Harebell Creek to its end near Crooked Creek is a series of ups and downs, switchbacks, and seemingly endless river crossings that will test your mettle. Buy a good compass, a topographical map, and a first-aid kit. Get yourself in good physical shape, then consult a backcountry ranger about this hike.

Solution Creek (Map 8)

CUTTHROAT

This is the outlet of Riddle Lake and a tributary to the West Thumb of Yellowstone Lake. Eight-inch cutthroat trout use the outlet near Riddle Lake, and large Yellowstone Lake cutts use the lower end of the creek for spawning. The creek is reached by following the 2½-mile trail east to Riddle Lake, then traversing the north shore to reach the stream on the east. The trailhead is a little more than 2 miles south of Grant Village, on the West Thumb–South Entrance Highway. Also see *Riddle Lake*.

Surprise Creek (Map 9)

CUTTHROAT

This small tributary to Outlet Creek holds small cutthroat trout. The "surprise" here is why anyone would want to fish a trailless canyon stream for small trout in the middle of grizzly country.

Thorofare Creek (Map 9)

CUTTHROAT

Located at the utmost end of the Thorofare Trail, 30 miles south of Lake Butte in the southeast corner of Yellowstone Park, Thorofare Creek is a major tributary to the Yellowstone River. There's excellent fishing for both spawning and resident cutthroats that average 15 inches, and it's located in the most wild and remote country left in the continental United States. The 60-mile round trip through the Thorofare's grizzly country deters most people, but if you have the time you'll be rewarded by sights and sounds few others will ever know.

Trail Creek (Map 9)

CUTTHROAT

This creek forms both the inlet and outlet of Trail Lake before it flows into the south arm of Yellowstone Lake. Trail

Creek is used primarily as a spawning stream for Yellowstone Lake cutthroats. It's reached by hiking 20 miles south from Lake Butte on the Thorofare Trail, then 2 miles east on the Trail Creek Trail.

Trappers Creek (Map 9)

CUTTHROAT

Flowing west into the Yellowstone River, 23 miles south of Lake Butte on the Thorofare Trail, Trappers Creek has a resident population of small cutthroats that share the stream with spawning trout from Yellowstone Lake. Resident fish average 8 inches, while the spawners might go to 16 inches. The spawners here and in other area streams begin returning to Yellowstone Lake by mid-July.

Witch Creek

Fishless. A small tributary to Heart Lake, Witch Creek drains many geothermal features.

LAKES AND PONDS

Alder Lake (Map 8)

CUTTHROAT

This 123-acre lake is located on The Promontory, the peninsula that separates the south and southeast arms of Yellowstone Lake. The Promontory is trailless, and hikers seldom fish this lake. The Trail Creek Trail provides the closest access, but it's still a 4-mile overland hike north from the trail to the lake. Alder contains a good population of cutthroat trout that average nearly a foot in length, but the warmth of summer months brings on an increase in algae growth, and by late July the lake's water is as green as its abundant lily pads. This is an interesting side trip, but it isn't a fishing destination.

Aster Lake

Fishless.

Basin Creek Lake (Map 9)

CUTTHROAT

This tiny eight-acre lake is best reached by following the South Boundary Trail 6 miles east, then heading 5 miles north on the Heart Lake Trail. The lake has fair fishing for small cutthroat trout.

Delusion Lake

Fishless.

Eleanor Lake (Map 8)

CUTTHROAT

Located 8½ miles west of the East Entrance, on the south side of the Fishing Bridge–East Entrance Highway, this shallow, two-and-a-half-acre pond contains a fair population of cutthroat trout that average 10 inches. Due to its location right off the highway, it receives a lot more fishing pressure than is warranted by the numbers and sizes of its fish.

Forest Lake

Fishless.

Glade Lake

Fishless.

Heart Lake (Map 9)

CUTTHROAT • LAKE TROUT • MOUNTAIN WHITEFISH

The Heart Lake Trailhead is 7½ miles south of West Thumb, on the West Thumb–South Entrance Highway. For the first 5 miles the trail winds at a gentle pace through lodgepole pines. It then descends to Witch Creek and through a meadow for its last 2½ miles. This 2,150-acre lake holds cutthroat and lake trout that average 18 inches. Mountain whitefish are also present, but they aren't as large. Anglers willing to pack in a float tube will do best, but you can also wade from shore. Sight casting to cruising or rising trout can be effective when the cutthroats are feeding on caddis or *Callibaetis* mayflies. If you're after lake trout, we suggest a sinking line and a size-2 streamer that imitates a cutthroat. The largest lake trout ever caught in the Park—43 pounds—was landed here.

Indian Pond (Map 8)

CUTTHROAT

Twenty-four-acre Indian Pond is located 3 miles east of Fishing Bridge, on the south side of the Fishing Bridge–East Entrance Highway. In 1880, then-Superintendent Norris named this lake "Indian Pond"; in the 1920s the name was changed to "Squaw Lake," and in 1981 it was restored to its original form. Older maps may still be labeled "Squaw Lake." Due to poor spawning habitat, the small cutthroats that live here provide poor fly fishing.

Mariposa Lake (Map 9)

CUTTHROAT • RAINBOW TROUT

It's a long hike into this 12-acre lake. Follow the South Boundary Trail east for 28 miles, and you'll find good fishing for 11-inch cutthroat, rainbow, and cuttbow hybrid trout. This is too far into grizzly country for us to recommend it, however.

Outlet Lake (Map 9)

CUTTHROAT

This 16-acre cutthroat lake, located 4 miles east of Heart Lake, is the headwater of Outlet Creek. Follow the Heart Lake Trail to Heart Lake, where it connects with the Trail Creek Trail. Take the latter along Outlet Creek until you reach Outlet Lake—a total distance of 15 miles from the trailhead to the lake. Small cutthroat trout and a long hike entice few anglers.

Riddle Lake (Map 8)

CUTTHROAT

Legends say that the waters of a lake on the Continental Divide flowed to both the Pacific and Atlantic Oceans, but its location was unknown—a "riddle." The location of the mysterious lake remains a mystery, so this lake, lying just east of the Continental Divide, was named "Riddle Lake." Its outlet flows in just one direction, however—east to the Atlantic. With this the riddle was solved, and the outlet of Riddle Lake became known as "Solution Creek."

This 274-acre lake is reached by a 2½-mile hike east on the Riddle Lake Trail, which begins a little more than 2 miles south of Grant Village, on the West Thumb–South Entrance Highway. The lake offers catch-and-release fishing for cutthroats that average 14 inches. The 45-minute hike to this beautiful lake is through grizzly country, so take precautions. *Callibaetis* mayflies bring fine rises of trout in July and August.

Sheridan Lake (Map 9)

CUTTHROAT

Located 11 miles southeast on the Heart Lake Trail, about 1 mile south of Heart Lake's south shore, Sheridan Lake is a marginal cutthroat fishery and not worth the hike.

Sylvan Lake (Map 8)

CUTTHROAT

Twenty-eight-acre Sylvan Lake is accessible right off the Fishing Bridge–East Entrance Highway, 10 miles west of the East Entrance. There's heavy fishing pressure here, but anglers can do well on this narrow lake by wading out and casting *Callibaetis* imitations to cruising trout gulping in the naturals. The lake opens to catch-and-release fishing on July 15, just about the time the *Callibaetis* hatch begins each summer.

Trail Lake (Map 9)

CUTTHROAT

Cutthroats averaging 16 inches are easily caught on this shallow, 55-acre lake located deep in the heart of grizzly country. Trail Lake is reached by following the Thorofare Trail 20½ miles south from Lake Butte to the Trail Creek Trail. Take the latter west for 2 miles and you'll cross Trail Creek itself. You'll have to hike the creek upstream for a mile until you reach the lake.

Yellowstone Lake (Map 8)

CUTTHROAT • LAKE TROUT

If you can't find this 87,450-acre lake on a map, you might consider politics as a career. Only the 31 miles of the west and north shorelines have road access. More than 80 miles of shoreline are accessible only by boat or by hiking one of the two trails that provide access. The Thorofare Trail runs along the east shore of the lake and is located 10 miles east of Fishing Bridge, on the East Entrance Highway. The Heart Lake Trail, located 7½ miles south of West Thumb, on the South Entrance Highway, provides access to the south and southeast arms of the lake. The Heart Lake Trail meets the Trail Creek Trail at the southeast corner of Heart Lake. Trail Creek Trail then meets the Thorofare Trail at the

Yellowstone Lake

southeast arm of Yellowstone Lake; this completes a loop around the lake.

Yellowstone Lake is the world's largest wild cutthroat fishery. This fishery was in jeopardy prior to 1975, when the population reached an all-time low. Then a limit of two fish, a minimum of 13 inches long, was instituted to protect spawning-sized cutthroat. Now it's difficult to catch a cutthroat of under 13 inches; most of the fish are larger. This foresighted management has returned cutthroat numbers to historic levels, providing a quality fishery that will last for years.

The lake opens to fishing June 15. Cutthroat trout are found in the shallow water along the lake's shoreline, where aquatic vegetation and insect life flourishes in this otherwise deep, ice-cold environment. Anglers can fish either from shore or from a float tube; there's no need for a boat.

The most popular place to fish is the Bridge Bay–Gull Point area—about 2 miles of shoreline next to the road on the west side of the lake. The other 29 miles of highway access receive little attention.

Gull Point is one of our favorite places to fish the lake. *Callibaetis* begin hatching around July 4. Since they seldom emerge before 10 A.M., we can have a leisurely breakfast at the Lake Hotel and still arrive at the lake in plenty of time. We get our tubes ready to go, but we begin by fishing nymphs from the shore to trout patrolling the shoreline. These fish know when a hatch is imminent. Initially they feed on *Callibaetis* nymphs, but they switch to duns as the hatch progresses. Once the fish make the switch, we climb into our tubes and follow into deeper water, where the fish tend to take the duns more readily. Tubes help us take advantage of the best morning and early-afternoon fishing.

As with tubing on any lake, be conscious of wind direction and speed to avoid being blown away from shore and having to fight your way back in.

The fishing is as easy as it sounds for the adventurous angler. With 31 miles of roadside access from which to choose (and another 80 backcountry miles), you don't have to see another angler unless you want to.

SELECTED EMERGENCES

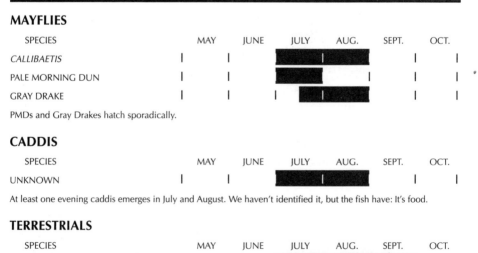

MAYFLIES

SPECIES	MAY	JUNE	JULY	AUG.	SEPT.	OCT.
CALLIBAETIS						
PALE MORNING DUN						
GRAY DRAKE						

PMDs and Gray Drakes hatch sporadically.

CADDIS

SPECIES	MAY	JUNE	JULY	AUG.	SEPT.	OCT.
UNKNOWN						

At least one evening caddis emerges in July and August. We haven't identified it, but the fish have: It's food.

TERRESTRIALS

SPECIES	MAY	JUNE	JULY	AUG.	SEPT.	OCT.
ANTS, BEETLES, AND GRASSHOPPERS						

SELECTED FLY PATTERNS

MAYFLIES

CALLIBAETIS

       HARE'S EAR FLASHBACK NYMPH, #14–#16

       CALLIBAETIS THORAX DUN AND HACKLE FIBER DUN, #16

       PARACHUTE ADAMS, #16

PALE MORNING DUN (PMD)

       PHEASANT TAIL NYMPH, #18

       PMD SPARKLE DUN, #18

GRAY DRAKE

       PARACHUTE ADAMS, #12

       HACKLE FIBER SPINNER, #14

CADDIS

       X-CADDIS OR ELK HAIR CADDIS, TAN, #14–#16

TERRESTRIALS

       DAVE'S HOPPER, #14

       FUR ANT, BLACK, #16–#18

       FOAM BEETLE, #12–#16

SCUDS AND LEECHES

       YELLOWSTONE SCUD, OLIVE, #14–#16

       YELLOWSTONE LEECH, BLACK, BROWN, OLIVE, #2–#10

       CRYSTAL BUGGER, BLACK, BROWN, OLIVE, #6

4

SOUTHWEST

FIREHOLE AND BECHLER RIVERS, NEZ PERCE CREEK, AND LEWIS LAKE

The southwest corner of the Park is characterized by spectacular geysers, lakes, and waterfalls. Most access is by hiking trail rather than by automobile, and in its remote reaches this area is lightly visited. Bison, elk, bears, moose, deer, and numerous species of birds may be your only companions.

Geysers line the banks of the Firehole River and some of its tributaries. These mineral-rich waters make for prolific mayfly and caddis hatches, which produce the most consistent dry-fly fishing in Yellowstone. Anglers from all over the world travel here to fish these hatches in the spring and fall.

Lewis and Shoshone Lakes offer anglers the best trophy-trout fishing in the Park. Large brown and lake trout are taken, from ice-out in June to the season's closure at the end of October. In late autumn, wading anglers can take large, aggressive brown and lake trout from the Lewis River Channel between the lakes.

The Cascade Corner of the Park, home to the Bechler and Falls Rivers, offers good fishing and fabulous scenery, including 21 of the Park's waterfalls. The features in this corner of Yellowstone can only be reached by trail. You have to *want* to be there to get there. That's why we go there.

RIVERS AND STREAMS

Arnica Creek (Map 11)

CUTTHROAT

This Yellowstone Lake tributary is 5⅓ miles north of West Thumb, on the West Thumb–Fishing Bridge Highway. Yellowstone Lake cutthroats use this creek as a spawning stream, but otherwise it isn't a viable fishery.

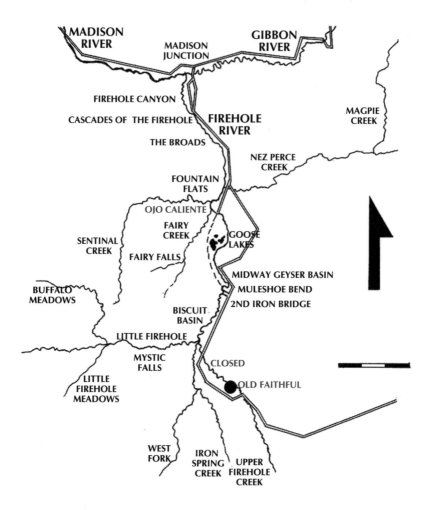

MADISON RIVER

GIBBON RIVER

MADISON JUNCTION

FIREHOLE CANYON

MAGPIE CREEK

CASCADES OF THE FIREHOLE

FIREHOLE RIVER

THE BROADS

NEZ PERCE CREEK

FOUNTAIN FLATS

OJO CALIENTE

FAIRY CREEK

GOOSE LAKES

SENTINAL CREEK

FAIRY FALLS

MIDWAY GEYSER BASIN

MULESHOE BEND

BUFFALO MEADOWS

2ND IRON BRIDGE

BISCUIT BASIN

LITTLE FIREHOLE

MYSTIC FALLS

CLOSED

LITTLE FIREHOLE MEADOWS

OLD FAITHFUL

WEST FORK

IRON SPRING CREEK

UPPER FIREHOLE CREEK

Map 10 — Firehole River

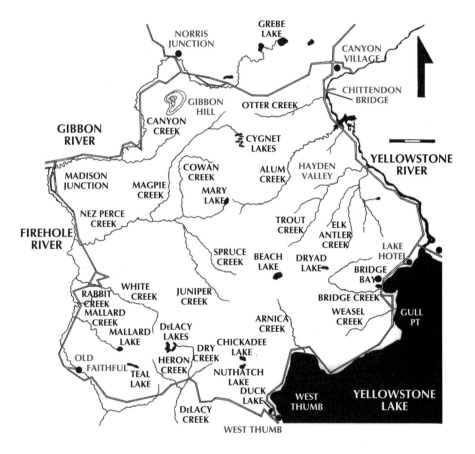

Map 11 — Nez Perce River

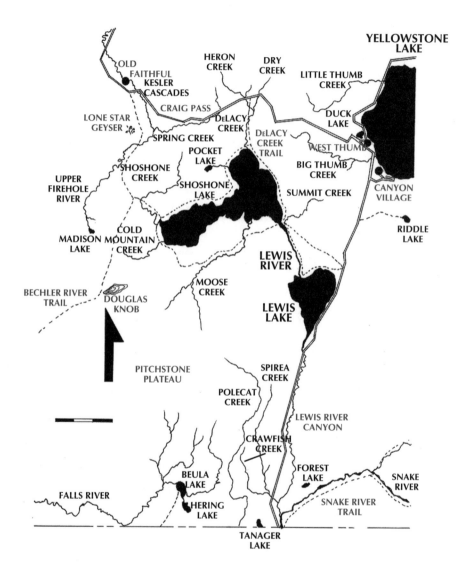

YELLOWSTONE
LAKE

OLD
FAITHFUL
KESLER
CASCADES

HERON
CREEK

DRY
CREEK

LITTLE THUMB
CREEK

CRAIG PASS

DUCK
LAKE

LONE STAR
GEYSER

DeLACY
CREEK

DeLACY
CREEK
TRAIL

WEST THUMB

SPRING CREEK

POCKET
LAKE

BIG THUMB
CREEK

SHOSHONE
CREEK

SHOSHONE
LAKE

SUMMIT CREEK

CANYON
VILLAGE

UPPER
FIREHOLE
RIVER

RIDDLE
LAKE

COLD
MADISON MOUNTAIN
LAKE   CREEK

LEWIS
RIVER

BECHLER RIVER
TRAIL

DOUGLAS
KNOB

MOOSE
CREEK

LEWIS
LAKE

PITCHSTONE
PLATEAU

SPIREA
CREEK

POLECAT
CREEK

LEWIS RIVER
CANYON

CRAWFISH
CREEK

BEULA
LAKE

FOREST
LAKE

SNAKE
RIVER

FALLS RIVER

HERING
LAKE

SNAKE RIVER
TRAIL

TANAGER
LAKE

Map 12 — Lewis Lake

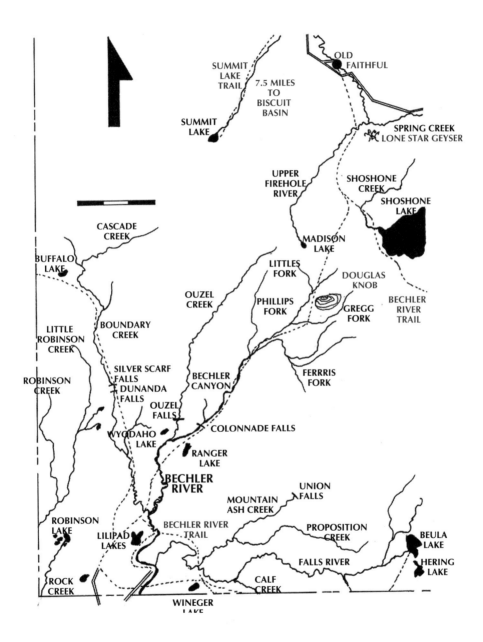

Map 13 — Bechler River

Bechler River (Map 13)

CUTTHROAT • RAINBOW TROUT

Most anglers don't think of the Bechler River as part of Yellowstone Park. In fact, few anglers think of the Bechler at all! Its only access is via Highway 47, which runs from Ashton, Idaho, to Cave Falls in the southwest corner of the Park. Compared to other rivers in Yellowstone, the journey to the Bechler is a commitment because it's so far off the beaten path. The river does, however, see a fair amount of traffic from local fishers.

The Bechler begins just north of Pitchstone Plateau, on the Pacific side of the Continental Divide. Just over the divide to the east is Shoshone Lake. The river flows southwest through long, narrow Bechler Canyon, picking up water from small tributaries and numerous hot mineral springs. Small cutthroats live in the canyon, but this place is strictly for backpackers—too far out of the way to make a fishing trip worthwhile.

The canyon ends about a mile below two-part Colonnade Falls. The upper falls drops 35 feet; the lower, 67 feet. Bechler Meadows begins where Ouzel Creek spills over 230-foot Ouzel Falls to join the Bechler River. The river winds back and forth constantly in this 4-mile-long meadow section, and there are few trees to block visibility; it's lined mostly by small willows. The water is crystal clear, with deep pools, undercuts, and overhanging grasses. Trout tend to hold in midstream, totally exposed in the gin-clear water. Just raising your rod tip can send them bolting for cover.

Fish range from 8- to 10-inch rainbows and cutthroats to a few that are very large. The secret to catching these fish is to spot them before they spot you. Once you locate one, you'll need to crawl on your hands and knees before casting. Usually, one cast is all you'll get, so be patient and don't hurry your presentation. One good cast can make your whole day.

We've seined the river and found a variety of insect life. This is the only water in Yellowstone Park that gets all the big Drakes—Brown, Gray, and Green. The Drakes bring up the big fish, and we make it a point to fish these early-season hatches. On the downside, mosquitoes and biting flies are merciless at this time. Long-sleeved shirts, head nets, and plenty of bug dope are mandatory to deter these bloodthirsty marauders. The swampy meadows, which don't dry until August, are another of the obstacles that make reaching the stream a downright chore. Therefore, most anglers choose to drum up trout with terrestrials in mid-August, when the meadows are dry and the biting-bug populations have diminished.

Bechler River

At the bottom of Bechler Meadows, you have two choices. The Bechler Meadows Trail leaves the river at this point, and the hike will take you back through the woods to the ranger station. There's no fishing along this trail. If you stay along the river, heading downstream, you'll come to the confluence of Boundary Creek and the Bechler River. The water is deep and cold, but it must be forded, as there's no bridge (the only bridge is upstream on the Bechler Meadows Trail, a mile out of the way). After crossing, you'll be on the Bechler River Trail, which follows the Bechler River down to its confluence with the Falls River, a distance of about 3 miles. There are some large fish in this stretch, but they're extremely scattered, and trying to find one is an all-day proposition. The river is mainly shallow riffles with a few pockets that hold small trout. While fishable, we can't recommend it.

The Bechler River ends at its junction with the Falls River, but the trail continues for a little less than a mile, ending at Cave Falls. Even though a trip to the Bechler involves a long hike, the trail is relatively flat and easy. Be sure to check trail conditions at the ranger station before making the hike.

Baetis Nymph

Tricorythodes Spinner

SELECTED EMERGENCES

MAYFLIES

SPECIES	MAY	JUNE	JULY	AUG.	SEPT.	OCT.
BAETIS			████████████████████			
PALE MORNING DUN			██████			
BROWN DRAKE			███			
GREEN DRAKE			███			
GRAY DRAKE				██████		
CALLIBAETIS				██████		
MAHOGANY DUN					████	
TRICORYTHODES					████	

CADDIS

SPECIES	MAY	JUNE	JULY	AUG.	SEPT.	OCT.
BRACHYCENTRUS					████	
HYDROPSYCHE			███			
HELICOPSYCHE		████████████████████████				
DICOSMOECUS					████	

STONEFLIES

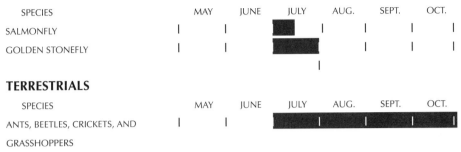

SPECIES		MAY	JUNE	JULY	AUG.	SEPT.	OCT.
SALMONFLY		|	|	▆	|	|	|	|
GOLDEN STONEFLY		|	|	▆	|	|	|
				|			

TERRESTRIALS

SPECIES		MAY	JUNE	JULY	AUG.	SEPT.	OCT.
ANTS, BEETLES, CRICKETS, AND		|	|	▆▆▆▆▆▆▆▆▆▆▆▆▆▆			
GRASSHOPPERS							

SELECTED FLY PATTERNS

MAYFLIES

BAETIS

PHEASANT TAIL NYMPH, #18–#22

6X EMERGER, #18–#22

BAETIS SPARKLE DUN, #18–#22

PALE MORNING DUN (PMD)

PMD EMERGER, #16

PMD SPARKLE DUN, #16

PMD SPINNER, #16

GREEN DRAKE

GREEN DRAKE EMERGER, #12

GREEN DRAKE PARADRAKE, #12

BROWN DRAKE

BROWN DRAKE SPARKLE DUN, #12

BROWN DRAKE SPINNER, #12

GRAY DRAKE

GRAY DRAKE SPARKLE DUN, #12

GRAY DRAKE SPINNER, #12

CALLIBAETIS

CALLIBAETIS SPARKLE DUN, #16

CALLIBAETIS SPINNER, #16

MAHOGANY DUN

MAHOGANY EMERGER, #16

MAHOGANY SPARKLE DUN, #16

TRICORYTHODES

TRICO SPARKLE DUN, #20–#22

CADDIS

BRACHYCENTRUS

PEACOCK & STARLING, #14–#16

X-CADDIS, OLIVE, #14–#16

HYDROPSYCHE

IRISE HYDROPSYCHE, #17

X-CADDIS, TAN, #16

SPENT CADDIS, TAN, #16

DICOSMOECUS

ELK HAIR CADDIS, ORANGE, #8

KAUFMANN'S STIMULATOR, ORANGE, #8

STONEFLIES

SALMONFLY

HENRY'S FORK SALMONFLY, #4–#6

GOLDEN STONEFLY

HENRY'S FORK GOLDEN STONEFLY, #6–#8

TERRESTRIALS

FOAM OR FUR ANT, BLACK, #14–#20

PARACHUTE AND DAVE'S HOPPERS, #8–#14

FOAM BEETLE, STANDARD, TIGER, #12–#18

SLOUGH CREEK CRICKET, #6–#8

Boundary Creek (Map 13)

CUTTHROAT • RAINBOW TROUT

This tributary to the Bechler River is reached by following the Boundary Creek Trail north for 5 miles from the Bechler ranger station. The Boundary Creek Trail and the Bechler Meadows Trail are essentially the same trail for the first 1¼ miles. The creek's lower section is better reached by sticking to the Bechler Meadows Trail. It's best to fish this creek in August; the trail remains muddy until then, and the mosquitoes are unbearable. Cutthroats, rainbows, and their hybrids can go as large as 14 inches, but the average size is under 10 inches. Terrestrial patterns are a must for this stream.

Boundary Creek

Bridge Creek (Map 11)

CUTTHROAT

This small creek flows into Bridge Bay off the West Thumb–Fishing Bridge Highway. It's a spawning stream for Yellowstone Lake cutthroats, and that's about it. Its mouth at Bridge Bay is closed to fishing.

Calf Creek (Map 13)

CUTTHROAT

This small tributary to the Falls River is reached either by a 7-mile hike east from Cave Falls on the South Boundary Trail, or by taking the primitive reclamation road west from Flagg Ranch, which is just south of the Park's South Entrance. Either way, the 7-inch cutthroats and rainbows aren't worth the trip.

Cascade Creek (Map 13)

CUTTHROAT

In our opinion, the minute trout in this tiny tributary to Boundary Creek, near Buffalo Lake, aren't a viable fishery.

Cold Mountain Creek (Map 12)

BROOK TROUT

There's no reason to fish for the small brook trout in this tributary to Shoshone Lake unless you're already there.

Cowan Creek (Map 11)

BROOK TROUT • BROWN TROUT • RAINBOW TROUT

This tributary to Nez Perce Creek offers poor fishing for small brook, brown, and rainbow trout. Access is by following the Mary Mountain Trail 7 miles east from the trailhead, located 6½ miles south of Madison Junction on the Madison–Old Faithful Highway.

Crawfish Creek (Map 12)

CUTTHROAT

This small tributary to the Lewis River is located on the west side of the South Entrance–West Thumb Highway, 1½ miles north of the South Entrance. Crawfish Creek's Moose Falls is far more spectacular than its 6- to 7-inch cutthroats.

DeLacy Creek (Map 12)

BROOK TROUT • BROWN TROUT

The 3-mile-long DeLacy Creek Trail parallels the fishable lower stretch of this small creek, which flows into the north shore of Shoshone Lake. The trailhead is 8 miles east of Old Faithful on the Old Faithful–West Thumb Highway. How small are the brook and brown trout here? A friend once used his wife's long blond hair as tippet material to land some. If you hunt for them, you can find resident fish of up to 7 or 8 inches.

Dry Creek

Fishless.

Fairy Creek (Map 10)

BROOK TROUT • BROWN TROUT • RAINBOW TROUT

This small meadow creek enters the Firehole River from the south, just across the river and downstream from the Ojo Caliente hot spring. Turn west on the Fountain Flats Freight Road, located 5½ miles south of Madison Junction. The road is closed after ¾ mile, so you must walk the remaining mile along the old service road to reach the Fairy Creek Trailhead. There are sparse populations of brook, brown, and rainbow trout, 8 inches and smaller.

Falls River (Map 13)

BROOK TROUT • CUTTHROAT • RAINBOW TROUT

This is the major river that drains the southwest, or Cascade Corner, of Yellowstone Park. Follow the South Boundary Trail east from Cave Falls to reach the lower river. To get to the upper river, take the reclamation road west from Flagg Ranch, which is located just south of the Park's South Entrance. The South Boundary Trail doesn't follow the river closely, so carry a compass and a topographic map if you decide to strike out on your own. Falls River has good fishing for rainbow and cutthroat trout, and they get larger the higher upstream you go. The long hike and off-trail access minimize fishing pressure.

Because it's easy to reach, the area near Cave Falls sees the most fishing. The trout average 10 inches in this stretch, and the action is good. To go upstream above Cave Falls, ford the river to reach the South Boundary Trail, about ½ mile south of Cave Falls. The stream leaves the trail and only comes close to it again in two places along its 30-mile length. The first is the Falls River Cutoff Trail, 4 miles east of Cave Falls. The second is where the Pitchstone Plateau Trail crosses the river, 8 miles east of Cave Falls. You'll be traveling through prime grizzly country; huckleberries and bears are a combination to look out for.

Beginning in July you'll see stoneflies, Pale Morning Duns, and Brown and Green Drakes. In September look for

Tricos, Gray Drakes, and Mahogany Duns. Otherwise, terrestrial species dominate here.

Ferris Fork (Map 13)

CUTTHROAT

One of the three sources of the Bechler River, Ferris Fork is located halfway between Cave Falls and Kepler Cascades on the Bechler River Trail. The other two sources are the Gregg and Phillips Forks. It's in heavily used bear country, but this fine stream has great fishing for 10-inch cutthroat. It also has three spectacular waterfalls: Ragged, Tendoy, and Wahhi Falls.

Firehole River (Map 10)

BROOK TROUT • BROWN TROUT • RAINBOW TROUT

Charlie Brooks called the Firehole River the "strangest trout stream on earth." Geysers, fumeroles, bubbling mud pots, and other such curiosities make this river one of the most interesting to fish. Arising from tiny, spring-fed Madison Lake as a small mountain creek, the Firehole makes its way north to Old Faithful, where it becomes a full-fledged trout stream. One-fifth of all the world's geysers are located within a mile of Old Faithful, pouring their mineral-rich thermal waters into the river and creating one of the world's classic limestone trout streams.

The river is closed to fishing in the vicinity of Old Faithful to protect the thermal features. It opens to fishing at Biscuit Basin, about 2 miles downstream of Old Faithful, where the road crosses the river. For the next 12 miles downstream to the Cascades of the Firehole, this is mostly a meandering meadow stream, with a few riffles thrown in for good measure. This stretch is Yellowstone's prime dry-fly water, with fine emergences of mayflies and caddis.

The river's brown and rainbow trout average 12 to 14 inches, with 16-inch fish not uncommon. Trout of over 20 inches are possible if you have the patience and nerve to

Firehole River

seek them out. These trout are known to be spooky during the prolific emergences of Pale Morning Duns and *Baetis* (Blue-Winged Olive) mayflies, as well as several species of caddis. The larger trout prefer to take up feeding lanes near the banks, shorelines, and weed beds, where the flies are concentrated. A stealthy approach upstream with long leaders and fine tippets comprises the recipe for success on this spring creek.

Matching the hatch is the most successful way to fool the larger trout in the smooth-water sections. During mayfly activity the fish will feed on all stages: nymphs, emergers, cripples, duns, and spinners. The same holds true for caddis periods: pupae, emergers, cripples, adults, and egg layers all draw the trout's attention.

It's hard to believe anyone could love this river more than we do. We live to fish the Firehole both spring and fall, exploring other streams in the Park during July and August,

Flav Spinner

Flav Nymph

when the Firehole's waters may climb into the 80s and force trout to seek relief in the cooler waters of its tributaries. No matter how much time we spend or experience we gain, though, we feel we're still learning to understand the complex moods of the Firehole.

About ½ mile downstream of the Firehole picnic area, the broad, smooth water changes pace. As the elevation drops and water speed increases, the river percolates over boulders and a rhyolite lava bottom, creating the Cascades of the Firehole. After 1½ miles the river leaves the road, heading west toward the 40-foot drop of Firehole Falls and the canyon. To get to this stretch, travel another mile north; a one-way road takes you back upstream through the canyon to Firehole Falls. This 1-mile stretch of water is a favorite of nymph and wet-fly fishers during the June salmonfly hatch and fall spawning run. This is your chance for a big, wild, Firehole River trout.

Below the canyon, the Firehole comes to an end at the junction pool where it merges with the Gibbon to create the Madison River.

The Firehole is unique. On no other river in the world will you experience this mix of superb fishing, geysers, and hot pots, with a chance to fish alongside elk, bison, and wolves.

SELECTED EMERGENCES

MAYFLIES

SPECIES	MAY	JUNE	JULY	AUG.	SEPT.	OCT.
BAETIS		██			████	
PALE MORNING DUN		███				
FLAV		██				

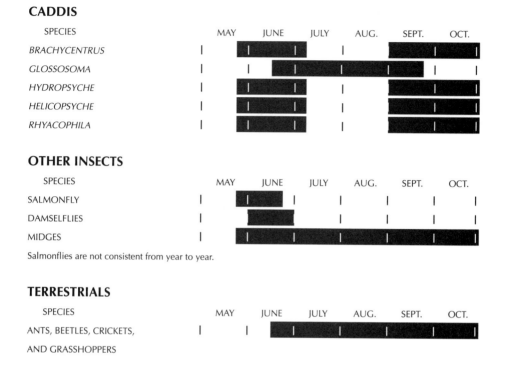

CADDIS

SPECIES	MAY	JUNE	JULY	AUG.	SEPT.	OCT.
BRACHYCENTRUS						
GLOSSOSOMA						
HYDROPSYCHE						
HELICOPSYCHE						
RHYACOPHILA						

OTHER INSECTS

SPECIES	MAY	JUNE	JULY	AUG.	SEPT.	OCT.
SALMONFLY						
DAMSELFLIES						
MIDGES						

Salmonflies are not consistent from year to year.

TERRESTRIALS

SPECIES	MAY	JUNE	JULY	AUG.	SEPT.	OCT.
ANTS, BEETLES, CRICKETS, AND GRASSHOPPERS						

SELECTED FLY PATTERNS

MAYFLIES

BAETIS

> PHEASANT TAIL NYMPH, #18–#22
>
> BAETIS SOFT HACKLE EMERGER, #20–#22
>
> BAETIS SPARKLE DUN, #18–#22
>
> BAETIS BIPLANE, #20–#22

PALE MORNING DUN (PMD)

> PMD NYMPH, #16
>
> PMD EMERGER, #16–#18
>
> PMD SPARKLE DUN, #16–#18
>
> PMD SPINNER, #16

FLAV

> PHEASANT TAIL NYMPH, #14
>
> EPHEMERELLA EMERGER, #14
>
> FLAV SPARKLE DUN AND SPINNER, #14–#16

CADDIS

BRACHYCENTRUS

    PEACOCK & STARLING, #14–#16

    ANTRON CADDIS PUPA, OLIVE, #16

    IRISE CADDIS, GREEN, #17

    X-CADDIS, OLIVE, #14–#16

    SPENT CADDIS, OLIVE, #16

GLOSSOSOMA

    PHEASANT TAIL SOFT HACKLE, #19

    X-CADDIS, BLACK, #20–#22

HYDROPSYCHE

    ANTRON CADDIS PUPA, AMBER, #14–#16

    IRISE CADDIS, GREEN AND TAN, #15–#17

    X-CADDIS, TAN, #16

HELICOPSYCHE

    X-CADDIS, AMBER, #20

RHYACOPHILA

    SERENDIPITY, LIME, #14–#16

    X-CADDIS, OLIVE, #14–#16

    SPENT CADDIS, OLIVE, #16

*Wetflies (from left):
Partridge and Primrose,
Peacock and Sterling,
6X Emerger,
Pheasant Tail Nymph,
Serendipity*

STONEFLIES

    BROOKS' BLACK STONE NYMPH, #4–#8

    KAUFMANN'S SEAL STONE, #4–#8

    HENRY'S FORK STONE, #4–#6

    KAUFMANN'S STIMULATOR, #4–#8

DAMSELFLIES

    HENRY'S LAKE DAMSEL NYMPH, #10–#12

    EXTENDED BODY ADULT DAMSEL, #10–#12

MIDGES

    SERENDIPITY, CRYSTAL, BROWN, OLIVE, #18–#22

    6X EMERGER, #20–#22

    Z-LON MIDGE, #20–#22

    GRIFFITH'S GNAT, #16–#20

TERRESTRIALS

    FUR OR FOAM ANT, #18–#20

    FOAM BEETLE, #14–#18

    DAVE'S HOPPER AND PARACHUTE HOPPER, #12–#14

Iron Spring Creek

Gregg Fork (Map 13)

CUTTHROAT

One of the three sources of the Bechler River, along with the Phillips and Ferris Forks, Gregg Fork lies on the Bechler River Trail midway between Cave Falls and Kepler Cascades. This small, remote creek has good fishing for cutthroats averaging 10 inches.

Heron Creek

Fishless.

Juniper Creek (Map 11)

BROOK TROUT • BROWN TROUT • RAINBOW TROUT

A tributary to Spruce Creek reached by the Mary Mountain Trail, Juniper Creek has poor fishing for tiny brook, brown, and rainbow trout.

Iron Spring Creek (Map 10)

BROOK TROUT • BROWN TROUT • RAINBOW TROUT

This medium-sized tributary enters the Firehole River immediately south of Biscuit Basin, 2¼ miles north of Old Faithful, near the Madison–Old Faithful Highway. There are resident populations of small brook, brown, and rainbow trout, plus a few good hatches of PMDs, BWOs, and caddis. The fish here are small until larger browns and rainbows from the Firehole move in to escape warm summer waters on the Firehole. These run-up fish are extremely difficult to approach; it's not unusual to spend the whole day here and catch only one. If that.

Lewis Channel (Map 12)

BROWN TROUT • LAKE TROUT

This 4-mile river channel, which connects Lewis and Shoshone Lakes, is considered the beginning of the Lewis River. The Lewis Channel Trailhead is located 7 miles south of West Thumb, on the West Thumb–South Entrance Highway. It's 3 miles to the point where the channel enters Lewis Lake, then another 4 miles to where the channel leaves Shoshone Lake, a total of 7 miles. Rather than hike the distance, many anglers prefer to take a motorboat across Lewis Lake to the channel and then hike to their favorite fishing spots.

There's not much happening in most of the Lewis Channel during the summer, except for canoe traffic paddling to Shoshone Lake. An exception comes in mid-June, when there's some lake-trout fishing where the channel enters Lewis Lake.

The prime fishing here is in October, specifically the last two weeks of the month. Brown trout and lake trout migrate into the channel and provide spectacular streamer fishing for truly large fish. We can still remember the snowy October days of 1983 when we accompanied Charlie Brooks and Dan Callaghan to the channel for their research on *Fishing*

Yellowstone Waters (Lyons & Burford, New York, 1984). It was the last time Charlie was able to make the trip. We'll never forget his nonstop ear-to-ear grin as Dan's motor-drive camera burned more than 30 rolls of film, photographing the colorful spawning brown and lake trout that Charlie landed.

Little Firehole River (Map 10)

CUTTHROAT • BROOK TROUT • BROWN TROUT • RAINBOW TROUT

This small tributary to the Firehole River enters from the west, immediately south of Biscuit Basin, 2¼ miles north of Old Faithful, near the Madison–Old Faithful Highway. Both the Little Firehole and Iron Spring Creeks enter the Firehole River in the same place. As you face west, the Little Firehole River is to your right, closer to Biscuit Basin; Iron Spring Creek is the one to the left. There are small resident brook, brown, rainbow, and cutthroat trout in the river. During the summer, larger fish from the Firehole move into the Little Firehole's cooler waters. Downed timber along the stream adds to the challenge of catching these fish.

Little Robinson Creek (Map 13)

BROOK TROUT

This tiny tributary to Robinson Creek enters 2 miles north of Robinson Lake. It has fair fishing for 8-inch brook trout near its confluence.

Littles Fork

Fishless.

Little Thumb Creek (Map 12)

CUTTHROAT

This small Yellowstone Lake tributary, located 2 miles north of West Thumb, is a spawning area for cutthroats and is closed to fishing at its mouth.

Mallard Creek

Fishless.

Magpie Creek (Map 11)

BROOK TROUT • BROWN TROUT • RAINBOW TROUT

This small tributary to Nez Perce Creek is reached by hiking the Mary Mountain Trail east for 5 miles. The trailhead is located 6½ miles south of Madison Junction, on the Madison–Old Faithful Highway. Magpie looks as though it should hold bigger fish than it does. Obvious undercuts, deep pools, and other favorable trout habitats are everywhere, but large fish are not. This is a pleasant hike, however, and the fishing is usually good for brook, brown, and rainbow trout. For no apparent reason, Magpie suffers year-to-year inconsistency.

Moose Creek (Map 12)

BROOK TROUT • BROWN TROUT

This small tributary enters Shoshone Lake from the south. Go west on the Lewis Channel Trail for 7 miles until you reach the outlet of Shoshone Lake. Ford the outlet and continue west, now on the Shoshone Lake South Shore Trail, for 2 miles, until you cross Moose Creek. This creek has good fishing for beautiful brown and brook trout that may reach 10 inches.

Mountain Ash Creek (Map 13)

BROOK TROUT • CUTTHROAT • RAINBOW TROUT

Mountain Ash Creek, a tributary to the Falls River, is reached by following the South Boundary Trail 4 miles east from Cave Falls to the Falls River Cutoff Trail. A 1½-mile hike north on the latter will bring you to the creek, which has fair fishing for cutthroat and rainbow trout averaging 8 inches. In September, there are some good hatches of Tricos and Mahogany Duns.

Nez Perce Creek (Map 11)

BROOK TROUT • BROWN TROUT • RAINBOW TROUT

A major tributary to the Firehole River, Nez Perce Creek enters the river at the Nez Perce picnic area, 5½ miles south of Madison Junction, on the Madison–Old Faithful Highway. Get to the best fishing by parking at the Mary Mountain Trailhead and hiking 2 miles to the bridge; this gets you above the geothermal features in Culex Basin. From the bridge upstream for 4½ miles to Spruce Creek, the fishing is good, mostly for brown trout, with an occasional rainbow or brook trout. This classic meadow creek is most productive during midsummer with terrestrials such as small grasshoppers and beetles. It's often closed due to bear and bison activity.

Ouzel Creek (Map 13)

CUTTHROAT • RAINBOW TROUT

This small tributary enters the Bechler River just below Bechler Canyon. Above Ouzel Falls it's fishless, but the ½ mile of stream below the falls has small cutthroat and rainbow trout. Enjoy the falls and fish the Bechler River instead.

Phillips Fork (Map 13)

One of the three sources of the Bechler River, Phillips Fork is located halfway between Cave Falls and Kepler Cascades on the Bechler River Trail. The other two sources are the Ferris and Gregg Forks. This beautiful little stream is fishless.

Polecat Creek (Map 12)

CUTTHROAT • BROWN TROUT

No trail leads into this small, mostly cutthroat fishery, but you will catch a lot of 6-inch fish here. Find Crawfish Creek and Moose Falls, 1½ miles north of the South Entrance, then hike off-trail 1 mile east to Polecat Creek.

Proposition Creek (Map 13)

CUTTHROAT

There's no trail along this small tributary to Mountain Ash Creek, and it offers less-than-fair fishing for 8-inch cutthroats. Once we took a 10-inch rainbow here, but we haven't seen another since 1989.

Rabbit Creek

Fishless.

Robinson Creek (Map 13)

BROOK TROUT • BROWN TROUT

Located on the West Boundary Trail, 3½ miles north of the Bechler River ranger station, Robinson Creek is full of brook and brown trout that average a plump 7 inches. Other than this pleasant fishery, the West Boundary Trail offers little in the way of sights and nothing in the way of fishing along its 36-mile length.

Rock Creek (Map 13)

BROOK TROUT

This is the outlet of Robinson Lake, located 2 miles north on the West Boundary Trail, on the west end of the lake. This trailless creek has marginal fishing for small brook trout; it's just not worth your time.

Shoshone Creek (Map 12)

BROOK TROUT • BROWN TROUT

This small tributary enters the southwest shore of Shoshone Lake west of the Cement Hills. Brook and brown trout that average 10 inches provide fun fly fishing for those who make the long hike: 8 miles southeast along the Shoshone Lake Trail, from Kepler Cascades to Shoshone Creek. Don't overlook the beautiful Shoshone Geyser Basin and the inlet to Shoshone Lake.

Spring Creek (Map 12)

BROOK TROUT • BROWN TROUT

This small creek enters the upper Firehole River about 2 miles upstream of Kepler Cascades, on the Lone Star Geyser Trail. A trail parallels the stream for about half its length, but the creek offers poor fishing for 6-inch brown and brook trout.

Spruce Creek (Map 11)

BROOK TROUT • BROWN TROUT • RAINBOW TROUT

Hike east on the Mary Mountain Trail for 6½ miles to find this small tributary to Nez Perce Creek. Spruce Creek has fair populations of brook, brown, and rainbow trout. They're small—6 to 7 inches—but the hike through the valley is lovely, with meadows filled with bright yellow cinquefoil and mariposa lilies.

Summit Creek (Map 12)

BROOK TROUT

This tiny tributary enters the Lewis River at the outlet of Shoshone Lake. Although there are tiny brook trout here, we don't consider this a viable fishery, especially with the Lewis Channel nearby.

Weasel Creek (Map 8)

CUTTHROAT

This tributary to Yellowstone Lake is located 6 miles south of Fishing Bridge near Bridge Bay. It provides marginal spawning habitat for Yellowstone Lake cutthroats but otherwise is not a viable fishery.

West Fork (Map 10)

BROWN TROUT • RAINBOW TROUT

This tiny tributary to Iron Spring Creek enters upstream of Black Sand Basin. There's no trail here, but there is poor fishing for 8-inch brown and rainbow trout.

White Creek (Map 11)

This tiny, thermal-fed tributary to the Firehole River is located across from the entrance to the Firehole Lake Loop Road, 8 miles south of Madison Junction, on the Madison–Old Faithful Highway. While some say this stream holds a population of brown trout, we've found no fish here.

LAKES AND PONDS

Beach Lake

Fishless.

Beula Lake (Map 12)

CUTTHROAT

This 107-acre cutthroat lake is near the south boundary of the Park, west of the South Entrance. You'll find the 2½-mile trail to the lake by driving west on the reclamation road from Flagg Ranch, 2 miles south of the entrance. It's a 9-mile drive west to the trailhead at Grassy Lake on this primitive road. Drive slowly and carefully. At Grassy Lake you'll see a small parking area on the north side of the road. An orange trail marker is posted on a tree.

Beula Lake is the headwater of the Falls River, and it has good fishing for cutthroats in the 12-inch range. You can fish the lake from shore, but a float tube makes things a little easier. A few inlets and springs enter the lake's south end, making this area marshy and difficult to navigate. One of these streams is the outlet from nearby Hering Lake. *Callibaetis* mayflies, caddis, and midges provide surface action in the summer. Otherwise, we recommend damselfly, dragonfly, and leech patterns for subsurface fishing.

Buffalo Lake

Fishless.

Chickadee Lake

Fishless.

Cygnet Lakes

Fishless.

DeLacy Lakes

Fishless.

Dryad Lake

Fishless.

Duck Lake

Fishless.

Feather Lake

Fishless.

Goose Lake (Map 10)

RAINBOW TROUT

This 34-acre lake is best reached by hiking the old Fountain Freight Road (closed to vehicles in 1996 and now referred to as the Fairy Falls Trail) from its south end at the second iron bridge, found 4½ miles north of Old Faithful, on the

Madison–Old Faithful Highway. There aren't many rainbow trout in the lake, and they're small, but they will rise to *Callibaetis* mayflies during July.

Gooseneck Lakes (Map 10)

RAINBOW TROUT

Unnamed on most maps, these small lakes are found atop the hills just west of Midway Geyser Basin. There's no trail up to the lakes, so you must hike the fishless outlet stream uphill. You'll find fair fishing for 8-inch rainbows.

Hering Lake (Map 12)

CUTTHROAT

This 60-acre cutthroat fishery, named for topographer Rudolph Hering of Hayden's second expedition, is found near the south boundary of the Park, close to Beula Lake. The best way to reach this lake is by following the directions to Beula Lake. Once at Beula, hike the shoreline to its southwest corner and locate the unmaintained trail that goes ½ mile south to Hering Lake.

Intermittent streams and rainfall are the sources of water for this lake, so annual precipitation will determine its actual size. During drought years the lake has been known to shrink to a quarter of its recorded acreage. The lake has good fishing for cutthroat trout, similar in most respects to Beula Lake, although the fish are smaller.

Isa Lake

Fishless.

Lewis Lake (Map 12)

BROOK TROUT • BROWN TROUT • CUTTHROAT • LAKE TROUT

A popular brown trout and lake-trout fishery, this 2,716-acre lake is found 12 miles north of the South Entrance, on

Lewis Lake

the West Thumb–South Entrance Highway. Campground and boat-launching facilities are located on the southeast side of the lake; this is the only lake besides Yellowstone Lake that allows motorized watercraft.

This is also the only lake we know of where you can catch brook trout, browns, cutthroats, and lake trout on a dry fly. Most of the angling pressure is from spin fishers, but a few local fly anglers make the lake a regular stop, fishing the drop-off along the southwest shore with sinking lines and leech imitations. The entrance to the lake's outlet is also a good place to land big trout on big dry flies, such as a size-8 Royal Wulff. Fishing from a tube or a boat is more reliable than wade fishing the outlet.

Streamers (clockwise from left):
Woolhead Sculpin,
Fly Fur Brown Trout,
Light Spruce

The best times to fish Lewis Lake are at ice-out in mid-June, warm summer evenings, and late October, when the spawning brown trout become aggressive. Stick with streamers and leeches in the early and late season, and look for caddis on warm summer evenings.

Lilypad Lake

Fishless.

Lower Basin Lake

Fishless.

Madison Lake (Map 13)

Headwater of the Firehole River. Fishless.

Mallard Lake

Fishless.

Mary Lake

Fishless.

Nuthatch Lake

Fishless.

Pocket Lake (Map 12)

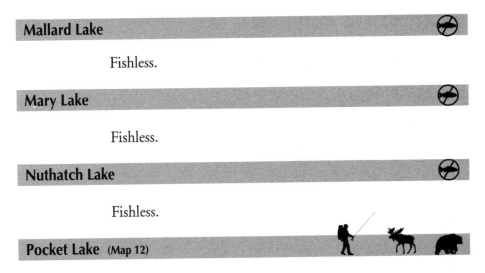

CUTTHROAT

This 14-acre lake sits in a "pocket" in the Cement Hills, above the northwest shore of Shoshone Lake. The lake is accessible over the 3-mile-long DeLacy Creek Trail, located 8 miles south of Old Faithful, on the Old Faithful–West Thumb Highway. Follow the trail to Shoshone Lake, then take a right on the Shoshone Lake North Shore Trail and walk about 2 miles. The outlet of Pocket Lake crosses the trail, and you'll have to hike the outlet up the ridge to the lake. Considering the hike, cutthroat trout in the 11-inch range make this a hard destination to recommend.

Ranger Lake (Map 13)

RAINBOW TROUT

Fifty-eight-acre Ranger Lake sits atop Pitchstone Plateau near the mouth of the Bechler River Canyon. It's an 8-mile hike along the Bechler River Trail, then a cross-country bushwhack up the ridge to the lake. We don't recommend the trip into this lake for its 10-inch rainbows.

Robinson Lake

Fishless.

Scaup Lake

Fishless.

Shoshone Lake (Map 12)

BROOK TROUT • CUTTHROAT • BROWN TROUT • LAKE TROUT

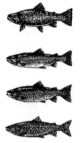

At 8,050 acres, Shoshone is the second largest lake in the Park and the largest lake in the continental United States that can't be reached by road. There are three practical routes for hiking in. The first two routes start at the Lewis Channel Trailhead, located 7 miles south of West Thumb on the West Thumb–South Entrance Highway. The Lewis Channel Trail is a 7-mile hike from the trailhead to the lake and is the most scenic route. The other trail is the Dogshead Trail to Shoshone lake, a shorter hike of 4½ miles that passes through Lodgepole Forest. The third choice is the DeLacy Creek Trail, located 9 miles west of West Thumb on the Old Faithful–West Thumb Highway. This 3-mile hike will take you to the north shore of Shoshone Lake.

Canoeing is allowed on Shoshone Lake. It's quite the saga to canoe and portage up the channel between Shoshone and Lewis Lakes, but it's well worth it once you arrive. Because of its remoteness and difficult access, Shoshone Lake receives little angling pressure. Brook trout from Moose Creek and cutthroats from nearby Pocket Lake are found here, but large brown and lake trout predominate.

Fishing begins here in mid-June, right after ice-out. Midges and *Callibaetis* can provide some good dry-fly action, while scud and leech imitations work well when there's no surface activity. Fishing slows in July and August, as the trout move to deeper, cooler water. Then you'll have to switch to sinking lines and big leech or baitfish imitations. Most anglers prefer to fish elsewhere in the Park at this time, returning to Shoshone Lake when the weather cools in September.

In late September, brown trout and lake trout migrate into the Lewis Channel to spawn. If you like to fish streamers, this is the time and place to land some truly big fish. See *Lewis Channel* for more information.

South Boundary Lake

Fishless.

Summit Lake

Fishless.

Tanager Lake

Fishless.

Winegar Lake

Fishless.

Wyodaho Lake

Fishless.

I N D E X